THE THINGS YOU THINK ABOUT
DETERMINE THE QUALITY OF YOUR MIND.
YOUR SOUL TAKES ON THE COLOR OF YOUR THOUGHTS.
– MARCUS AURELIUS

The Roman civilization was one of the greatest in world history. Its roots are deep in the past. How the City of Rome was founded is a mystery. It is impossible to separate truth from legend. Legend has it that Mars, the Roman god of war, had twin sons, Romulus and Remus. Their mother was a princess, Rhea Silvia, who lived in the town of Alba Longa in Italy. Rhea's evil uncle, who was a king, ordered that the twins be killed, and his servants left the babies to die on the bank of the Tiber river. They were found by a she-wolf, who protected and fed them until a shepherd came across her lair and adopted the two boys into his family.

When they grew up, Romulus and Remus decided to found their own city. The area that was to become Rome had seven hills. Romulus and Remus argued over which hill was the best place to start building their city. Their quarrel turned into a violent conflict between their supporters, and Remus was killed. Romulus founded the city on the Palatine Hill, named it Rome, and became its first king.

According to the legends, Rome was founded in 753 BC, and archaeologists agree that it was in the 8th century BC when the villages on the seven hills first blended into a city.

From the days of Romulus, Rome was ruled by kings for about 240 years. The kings did not inherit the kingdom, they were elected by *the Senate,* a group of royal advisors from the most powerful families of the city. These families were considered noble, or *patrician*. The language of ancient Rome was Latin. The word *patrician* comes from the Latin *patres conscripti* – enlisted fathers. It was a phrase describing Roman senators, who were enlisted to serve in the king's council.

'Shepherd Faustulus with Romulus and Remus'
by Nicolas Mignard

The families that were not *patrician* were called *plebeian* or *plebs* – which means *the people*. So Roman society was divided into patricians, plebeians, and slaves. The slaves were mostly prisoners of war who worked as servants, or farm and construction workers. About one-third of the Roman population were slaves.

The second king of Rome, after Romulus, was Numa Pompilius. Roman historians believed that he was Rome's wisest king. He taught the Romans to obey the law, respect marriage, family, religion, and education, to be kind to enemies who surrendered, and to value honor and patriotism. The people of Rome loved Numa's new laws and ideas. When asked how he thought of them all, Numa said that the nymph Egeria, the goddess of poplar trees, gave him advice and taught him how to be a wise ruler.

'Numa Consulting the Nymph Egeria'
by Jean Claude Naigeon

The 7th and the last Roman king was Tarquin the Proud. He reigned for 25 years. Legends say he was a cruel and lawless ruler who murdered his wife and his elder brother to gain the throne. Servius Tullius, who was the 6th king of Rome, ordered his two daughters to marry Tarquin and Tarquin's older brother. Roman women were usually given a name formed from their father's last name. So the two daughters of Servius Tullius were named Tullia. The older was *Tullia Major* (Big Tullia) and the younger was *Tullia Minor* (Little Tullia).

Tullia Minor, the wife of Tarquin's brother, wanted to become the Queen of Rome, but she thought her husband was not ruthless enough to rule. So Tarquin and Tullia Minor agreed to murder Tarquin's brother and Tullia's sister. They actually did it: They killed their brother and sister, and got married! Next, they plotted against King Servius, and when he was murdered, and his body was lying in the street, Tullia Minor rushed to the Senate house to greet her husband as the new king, rolling her chariot right over her dad's dead body. The street where this happened was named *Vicus Sceleratus* – the Street of Shame, and Tullia Minor's name became a synonym for greed and crime.

Tarquin's reign was full of crime, betrayals, and dishonesty. During a war with a nearby city, Tarquin told his son to pretend that he wanted to betray his father, go to the enemy city and win their trust. Once the enemies made Tarquin's son the leader of their army, he sent a messenger to Tarquin asking what to do next.

Bronze Roman helmet, 4th century BC

Tarquin received the messenger but didn't answer his question. "Instead," says the Roman historian Livy, "The king went into the palace garden, deep in thought, his son's messenger following him. As he walked along in silence he struck the heads off the tallest poppy flowers with his stick." Tarquin's son heard this story from the messenger and took the hint. He falsely accused the enemy city leaders of betrayal and had them beheaded. Soon the city surrendered to Rome.

In European literature and political culture the words *tall poppy* became a way to describe successful people who are resented, attacked, and undercut not because of any mistakes they had made, but because of envy for their success.

Needless to say, the people of Rome hated Tarquin, and after a few more lawless acts and betrayals, the Senate took away Tarquin's *imperium* – his authority to rule the people of Rome – and sent him into exile. Tarquin joined forces with nearby kingdoms and one after another three different armies marched on Rome, but all were defeated by the Roman citizens, and Tarquin died in exile.

'Tullia driving her chariot over her father' by Giuseppe Bartolomeo Chiari, 1687

In 509 BC Rome became a republic ruled by the Senate. The word republic comes from the Latin phrase *res publica* where *res* means 'thing,' and *publica* means 'belonging to the public.' Romans distinguished between private property – *res privata*, and public property – *res publica*, which was managed by the state. So at the time of the Roman republic *res publica* meant the state governed by elected officials. For almost 500 years, from 509 BC to 27 BC, Rome was a republic. During that period Rome grew from a small city in central Italy to the ancient world's most powerful civilization.

'Tarquin the Proud'
by Lawrence Alma-Tadema, 1867
Model of the Capitol – Capitoline Hill in Rome

Most of the political life in the Roman Republic revolved around the struggle between the patricians, the powerful families, and the plebeians, the common people. Cincinnatus was from a patrician Roman family. He served in the Roman Senate, but his family was not wealthy. His enemies falsely accused his son of crimes, and his family had to pay a huge fine. As a result they lost all their money, and Cincinnatus, already quite old, worked at a small farm he owned to make his living. His last name, Cincinnatus, means **curly haired** in Latin.

When a nearby city broke a peace agreement with Rome and attacked, the Roman Senate decided there was only one man who they all trusted to lead Rome into battle: Cincinnatus. They sent a couple senators to his farm. As they arrived, they saw him ploughing a field. Cincinnatus looked up and asked, "Is everything all right?" They told him to put on his senator's **toga** and be ready to hear the message they were carrying to him from the Senate of Rome.

'Cincinnatus leaves his farm' by Juan Antonio Ribera, and Roman vase, 330 BC

The Roman toga was a semicircular cloth from 12 to 20 feet long (4 to 6 meters long). It was made of white wool and was draped around the body over a tunic. The togas of high-ranking officials had a purple edge. Cincinnatus asked his wife Racilia to bring his senator's toga from the simple farm hut where they lived. He wiped off the dirt and sweat, put on his toga, and waited.

To his amazement, the Roman senators saluted him as *dictator*.

In the days of the *Respublica Romana*, or Roman Republic, a dictator was a person given unlimited power to rule Rome for 6 months. For example, in time of war, a dictator was a leader who had the authority of a king until peace returned.

Cincinnatus went to Rome, accepted his dictatorship, and led the Roman army to victory. When prisoners of that war were brought to the Roman camp, the Romans did not kill them, but made them pass under an arch of 3 spears as a promise that they would never attack the Romans again. Right after this victory, Cincinnatus returned to his farm and kept working in his fields. This was not the only time the Romans called on Cincinnatus to save them. It happened again, and both times Cincinnatus served the Roman state as their leader and then gave up his power once the war was won. He was always ready to help his country even though it didn't always treat him well. Cincinnatus didn't care about power and authority.

Cincinnatus was a favorite Roman hero of George Washington. As America's first president and general, Washington gave up his power at the end of his presidency and retired to his farm, just like Cincinnatus. In honor of Washington, the veterans of the American War of Independence created an organization they called Cincinnati which means 'belonging to Cincinnatus' in Latin. Cincinnati also became the name of a big city in the US state of Ohio.

'A Roman senator and his guest, with slaves attending' by Henryk Semiradzki

CORIOLANUS   5th century BC

Gaius Marcius Coriolanus was a Roman military leader who became famous in 493 BC during the war against the city of Corioli. Corioli was captured and Marcius gained the nickname Coriolanus.

Roman historian Plutarch writes that when Marcius was a young man, he participated in a battle where he "saw a Roman soldier struck down nearby. He ran to him at once, stood in front of him, defended him and saved his life." At the victory parade Marcius was crowned with a wreath of oak leaves. An oak-leaf crown was given to Roman citizens who saved the life of a fellow citizen in a battle. That was the beginning of Coriolanus' military career.

Like many Roman leaders before him, Coriolanus was on the side of the patricians against the plebeians. But plebeians were growing in power, and the plebeian enemies of Coriolanus falsely accused him of crimes against the state. Coriolanus was angry and refused to come to his trial. Next, afraid that he would be killed by his enemies, he left the city.

In 1605 the great English playwright William Shakespeare wrote a play he called *Coriolanus.* In this play, while saying good-bye to his enemies, Coriolanus says, "...I turn my back. There is a world elsewhere."

Angry at the Romans, Coriolanus considered betrayal. Roman historian Plutarch says that Coriolanus went to the house of Tullus, the leader of Volsci, the enemies of the Romans. He entered the house and sat by the fireplace covering his head with his cloak. "The people of the house were concerned," says Plutarch, "They told Tullus, and when Tullus asked him who he was, he said: "I am Gaius Marcius, and my surname is Coriolanus. I am an enemy to your people. I come here with a desire to take revenge on my enemies in Rome, and I put myself in your power. "

Before long, Coriolanus marched on Rome with a huge army. Rome had no hope. The Roman Senate sent their ambassadors to Coriolanus to try to negotiate peace. Coriolanus sent them back. Then, says Plutarch, the Romans sent all the priests of the gods dressed in their sacred clothes to beg Coriolanus to stop the war. Coriolanus sent them back with nothing. But there was a woman in Rome whose name was Valeria. She gathered some Roman women and brought them all to the house of Volumnia, the mother of Coriolanus.

'Coriolanus' by Nicolas Poussin, 1652

They entered the house and saw Volumnia and the wife of Coriolanus, Vergillia, playing
with his kids. Seeing them, Valeria said: "Dear Volumnia and Vergillia, we come to you
as women to women. We don't care for the orders of the Senate, but we know that gods have put
this desire in our hearts to save the citizens of Rome and win you the glory of making peace.
Come with us to Coriolanus, and join us in asking him on behalf of your country to make peace..."
"We'll go with you," said Volumnia, mother of Coriolanus, "and if nothing else, we can at least
breathe our last breath asking my son to be kind to our country."

After this, she took her daughter-in-law Vergilia and her grandkids and went with the other
women to the camp of Coriolanus. When the enemies saw the women, they felt sorry for the Romans
and for Coriolanus, and fell silent. Coriolanus greeted his mother and hugged her for a long time.
Then he hugged and kissed his wife and children. He was not ashamed to cry. When his mother
spoke to him, he listened without making any answer, and stood there, in front of her, for a long
time in silence. The next morning he led his army away from the walls of Rome and stopped
the war. After this, nothing more is known about the life of Coriolanus.

The Romans were so grateful to the women of the city that they built a beautiful temple in memory
of that event called The Temple of Women's Fortune.

CATO THE CENSOR

234 – 149 BC

In the 4th century BC Greek king Alexander the Great conquered nearly all of Southern Europe and created an empire that stretched from Africa to India. Greek settlements called 'colonies' and Greek culture spread all over the Mediterranean world. Even after Alexander's empire fell apart and Greece was weakened by internal wars, Greece was still the most important cultural influence across the whole of Western civilization. That era is often called the *Hellenistic period* from the word *Hellas* – Greece.

Ancient Rome borrowed most of its culture from Greece. The Greek gods were given Latin names and became Roman Gods: Zeus – Jupiter, Athena – Minerva, Aphrodite – Venus, Ares – Mars, and so on. Roman temples and public buildings used Greek styles of architecture. Roman literature, theater, sports, fashions - almost everything came from Greece.

Not all Romans, however, welcomed Greek culture. Marcus Porcius Cato was one of the Roman leaders who called upon the Roman nation to bring back the ancient culture and customs of Rome. He was a patrician, but he grew up on a farm where he worked with his hands. He joined the Roman army at 17, and became a war hero. He was elected a senator, then a *consul*, then a *censor*. Consuls were chairmen of the Senate, and censors counted the citizens during census and kept an eye on the people's public behavior.

Cato thought that fashion, home decoration, buying art, or cooking Greek dishes spoiled his fellow citizens and made them greedy and less patriotic. Once elected a censor, Cato made people pay a huge tax on any expensive or artistic object they owned, such as jewelry, fashionable clothes, even beautiful dishes or drinking cups in their homes!

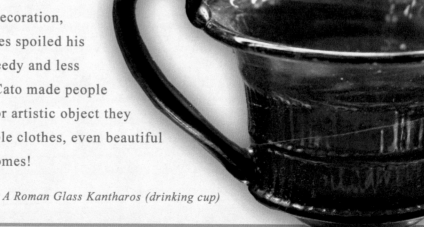

A Roman Glass Kantharos (drinking cup)

A lot of people felt that Cato was on the right track. They agreed that values such as honesty, patriotism, responsibility, and serving the people of your country were important. Most Romans also agreed that it was all right if a woman wore fashionable clothes and jewelry, but for a man it was not considered manly to buy trinkets and colorful clothes. However, many people also thought Cato went a little too far. What was wrong with eating from a plate painted by an artist, or reading Greek literature to your kids at bedtime?

Kids were a problem too, declared Cato. He believed that women and kids make their husbands and dads buy them all sorts of expensive gifts and exotic toys brought from faraway lands. Our republic rules half the world, he complained, but our wives and kids rule us! He often repeated the words of the Greek leader Themistocles who said to his wife: "Wife, the city of Athens rules Greece, I rule the city of Athens, you rule me, and our son rules you. Make sure that he doesn't overuse his authority which makes him, a little kid, the most powerful man in Greece." Many people came to hate Cato. They accused him of this and that, and he was forced to defend himself in court over 40 times! "Cato used to say that he preferred to do right and get no thanks, rather than to do wrong and get no punishment," says Plutarch, "and that he pardoned everybody's mistakes except his own."

'Scene of ancient Rome' by Prospero Piatti, and a Roman fresco, 50 BC

Also, Cato was a hard worker, generous with his knowledge and skills.

Plutarch describes Cato's work day: "In the morning Cato went on foot to the Forum and helped people who needed defense in court." The Forum was the square in Rome, where people met to discuss politics, business and the law. In the evening, says Plutarch, "Cato came back to his farm, where, dressed in simple clothes, he ploughed fields and gathered crops alongside his farm workers. In the evening he sat down with them to eat the same bread and drink the same wine."

Cato became famous for his speech-making talent. Many of his sayings were memorable. For example, once he opposed giving away grain to the people of Rome. He thought grain should be saved for harder times, so he started his speech with these words:

"It is a hard matter, my fellow citizens, to argue with the belly, since it has no ears."

He also said, "Wise men benefit more from fools than fools from wise men; because the wise learn from the mistakes of fools, but fools do not learn from the successes of the wise."

There were just as many people who admired Cato as those who hated him. One of his friends was upset that even though Cato was so famous, Romans hadn't made any statues of him. But Cato said, "I would much rather have men ask why I have no statue, than why I have one... My statues are in the hearts of my fellow citizens." He thought a good citizen should not even allow himself to be praised, unless that praise was good for his country.

Cato was a good father. He taught his son himself, giving him lessons in literature, law, horse riding, military skills, boxing, and swimming. He wrote a book of Roman history for his son. "He wrote it with his own hand," says Plutarch, "and in large characters, so that his son could read it and learn about his country's ancient traditions."

There was one more thing that made Cato famous. Whenever he made a public speech, he always ended it with the same words: ***Carthago delenda est.***

Translated from Latin, it's 'Carthage must be destroyed.'

"The City of Carthage" by Willian Turner

Carthage was a city in North Africa, and a center of the Punic Republic. It was founded by Phoenicians, people from the Levant, the area of modern Syria and Lebanon. They spoke the *Canaanite* (also known as *Punic*) language, related to such modern languages as Arabic and Hebrew. In the 3rd century BC Carthage and Rome clashed in a number of wars, known as the Punic wars, that lasted for over 100 years.

The Romans won the first Punic War thanks to their new military invention – the *corvus*. The Romans were not good at sea battles, but on land their soldiers were the best in the world. So they figured out how to turn a sea battle into a land battle. The corvus was a bridge that the Romans launched at an enemy ship. *Corvus* in Latin means 'raven.' It had a heavy spike shaped like a beak of a bird that anchored into the deck of an enemy ship and allowed Roman soldiers to board it and fight in the same way they fought on land. The Second Punic War, however, was disastrous for Rome. Only thanks to the military genius of the Roman general Scipio Africanus did Rome survive.

Publius Cornelius Scipio first fought against the Carthaginians when he was only 18. His father, a Roman consul, was surrounded by the Carthaginian troops in a battle. Scipio led Roman soldiers to break their circle and saved his dad.

But now the Romans were facing a new kind of enemy. Hannibal, a Carthaginian general and one of the greatest military commanders in history, came up with new, unheard-of strategies. He struck Italy from the North where he was least expected. Hannibal's army left Spain, went North, and crossed the Alps mountains. The Romans couldn't believe it. The Alps are high mountains with dangerous narrow passages. Nobody thought it was possible to cross the Alps with an army of thousands of men, horses, and even elephants that Hannibal brought with him from Africa. But Hannibal made it happen and now his troops occupied most of Italy.

A marble bust of Hannibal found in Italy

The Romans challenged Hannibal by the town of Cannae and were wiped out in one battle. Out of 87 thousand Roman soldiers only 10 thousand survived. 20-year-old Scipio was one of the Roman officers who led his soldiers to safety. Soon Scipio's father and uncle were defeated and killed fighting Hannibal's forces in Spain.

The Roman Senate voted to send troops to avenge the defeat, but none of Roman generals would agree to lead those troops! It was the same as a death sentence, they thought. Scipio was 25, too young to command a whole army, but since he was the only one who would take the job, the Senate agreed to send him to Spain.

Scipio was a fast learner. Having seen Hannibal's brilliant strategies in action, he started using he started using Hannibal's own methods against Carthage, winning one victory after another. By 206 BC he took the whole of Spain from the enemy, isolated Hannibal in southern Italy, and decided to take the war to Carthage itself by invading North Africa. However, many of Scipio's best officers and soldiers were poorly armed. In those days each soldier bought their own weapons. So people from wealthy families were better armed and had horses, but they were not necessarily the best soldiers. The Roman Senate didn't offer Scipio any help. He was only 31 and some older senators envied him.

In his "Nine Books of Memorable Deeds and Sayings" Roman historian Valerius Maximus writes that Scipio came up with a clever plan. He chose 300 young men from the wealthiest families of Sicily, and ordered them to get themselves the best armor, weapons, and horses. "You will be the first to storm Carthage with me," he told them. The young men were wondering, "Why did he choose us?" Some of them were a little scared, and their families were plain terrified. Once they were armed, Scipio told them that being the first to storm Carthage meant almost certain death, and if they wanted to offer their place to a more experienced soldier, they could do that if they gave the more experienced soldier their armor, weapons and a horse. Most of the 300 young men quickly offered their place to a more experienced soldier and in this way Scipio armed his best unit.

'Battle of Cannae' by John Trumbull, 1773

'Battle of Zama' by Cornelis Cort

Landing in Africa, Scipio's soldiers caught some Carthaginian spies and wanted to kill them, but Scipio stopped them. Valerius Maximus writes: "Scipio didn't put the spies to death, nor throw them in prison, nor even ask them any questions about the enemy. Instead he lined up his troops and had the spies take a look at every unit of his army. After that he gave them food for the road and let them go home to Carthage." Having heard the spies' report about the power of the Roman army, Carthaginians were in panic. Hannibal had to go home to defend Carthage. In 202 BC Hannibal's and Scipio's armies fought the famous Battle of Zama. Scipio won and ended the war. This victory won him the nickname Africanus.

Scipio became famous for his kind treatment of prisoners of war. Valerius Maximus says that among the Carthaginian prisoners there was a young lady who had become separated from her family and then captured by Roman troops. Her parents sent gold to Scipio as a ransom. But Scipio let her go home safely with all the gold. He didn't like to see innocent people suffer. The lady turned out to be a princess from Spain. Her family was so grateful, they joined Scipio's forces.

Negotiating peace with Carthage, Scipio was generous. He didn't allow his soldiers to plunder the conquered lands. He allowed Carthage to keep its territories in Africa. He pardoned Hannibal and all prisoners of war, and even let the city keep ten warships to protect its trade routes.

'Generosity of Scipio (Scipio and the Spanish Princess)' by Pompeo Battoni

Scipio returned home as a hero, but not everyone was happy with the peace agreement he made. Many Roman leaders suspected that Carthaginians had bribed Scipio. Maybe they just envied him, but Scipio had to defend himself against accusations of treason and corruption.

Not sure whether to thank Scipio or to attack him, the Senate offered to make him a consul and a dictator for life, and to put his statues on the Forum and in its Temples, but Scipio said no to all these honors.

Scipio's greatest enemy now was Cato. Cato couldn't stand Scipio, because Scipio lived the lifestyle of a wealthy Roman patrician. Scipio loved parties and feasts, wore expensive clothes and sandals, went to the gym every day to stay fit, and spent a lot of money on sports competitions and theater, while Cato worked with his hands on his own farm and dressed like his farm workers.

Valerius Maximus defends Scipio's expensive habits, saying that even though he wore soft clothes and shoes, he handled the Carthaginians without any softness in war. Scipio's family never lost the sight of real values. Valerius Maximus writes that when girlfriends of Scipio's daughter Cornelia asked her to show them her most precious jewels, she called her kids, and pointing at them said, "These are my jewels."

Sculpture from the 4th century BC found in Spain: *'Cornelia and her Jewels' by Elizabeth Jane Gardner Bouguereau*
Its style was influenced by the art of Carthage

Tired of accusations, Scipio left Rome and retired from public life. He lived in his countryside house until his death in 183 BC. He ordered that upon his death he should be buried not in Rome, but near his country house. The words on his grave said:

Ungrateful fatherland, you won't even have my bones.

Many years after Scipio died, in the Third Punic War, Rome attacked the city of Carthage, and after three years of siege, broke through the walls and burned Carthage to the ground.

'Scipio frees an enemy prince' by Giovanni Battista Tiepolo

POMPEY THE GREAT

Gnaeus Pompey's father was a general who perished in a battle when Pompey was 19. Pompey inherited his father's wealth and his legions. A *legion* was a unit of the Roman army made of 5000 soldiers and led by a *legate*. Each legion was divided into 10 *cohorts* of 500 men each, and each cohort had 5 *centuries*, units of 100 men led by *centurions*.

Still a teenager, Pompey was the commander of a well-trained and loyal army, but he was too young to be elected to the Roman senate and take part in the government. So he joined the Roman general and dictator Lucious Cornelius Sulla in Sulla's struggle for power. Sulla marched on Rome and seized it. Pompey became his right-hand man.

Soon Sulla sent Pompey to recapture Sicily and North Africa, and Pompey was so successful that his troops named him *Magnus* – the Great. While fighting in Africa, Pompey's troops met with an unexpected delay. Some of his soldiers stumbled upon a treasure that was buried in the ground near Carthage. When other soldiers heard about it, they figured that there must be more treasures hidden away by Carthaginians during the Punic Wars. As a result Pompey's army did nothing but hunt for treasures for days, and Pompey couldn't stop them. He laughed seeing thousands of men digging the ground all around Carthage. They didn't find much and ended up laughing at themselves. Soon Pompey's army moved on.

Sulla was so impressed with Pompey's victories, that when Pompey saluted him with the title of *Imperator*, he saluted Pompey in return as *Imperator* too. In the days of the Roman Republic the word *imperator* meant commander, not 'emperor.' It took Sulla many years and many victories to gain the title Imperator, so when he addressed Pompey that way, everyone knew Pompey's star was rising.

"A Roman Triumph" by Carle Vernet

After this, says Plutarch, Pompey asked the Senate for a ***triumph*** to celebrate his victories. A triumph was a victory parade held when a military commander returned to Rome with victory. It was a long procession. First in the triumphal procession came prisoners and captured enemy leaders with their families. Then came soldiers carrying the weapons of the defeated enemy, as well as their armor and treasures, such as gold, silver, and statues of the enemy gods. Next, on foot, came Roman senators and officials, and finally the war hero himself came riding a four-horse chariot. Sometimes his young kids rode with him in the chariot, while his officers and grownup sons rode horses alongside. Finally, the soldiers of the victorious army walked following their commander and wearing crowns made of laurel branches. They usually sang songs about the war they won, and a lot of those songs were making fun of their commander. The people of Rome laughed, cheered, and threw flowers at the soldiers and their general.

When Pompey asked for a triumph, Sulla said Pompey was too young to be elected even a senator. It was only consuls, the Senate leaders, who were allowed to have triumphs. Scipio Africanus didn't ask for triumphs when he was that young, said Sulla.

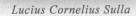

Lucius Cornelius Sulla

But Pompey was not going to be pushed around by some old general. "People prefer to worship the rising sun, not the setting sun," he said. Everyone who heard him gasped and looked at Sulla. Sulla was so shocked and amazed at the boldness of Pompey, that he cried out: "All right, let him triumph!"

There were many Romans who felt that young Pompey should be more modest, but the more they opposed him, the more Pompey wanted to annoy them. He had brought home a few elephants from Africa, and tried to ride into the city on a chariot drawn by four elephants instead of horses. But the gate of the city was too narrow, so he had to switch to horses after all!

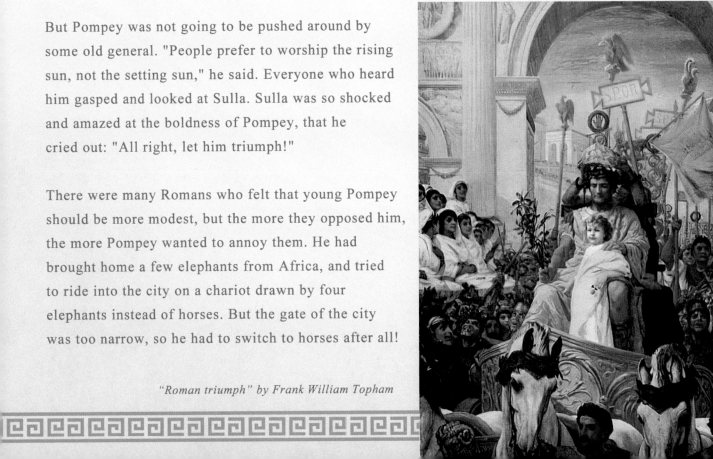

"Roman triumph" by Frank William Topham

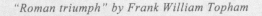

After his triumph, Pompey had many more military successes, including a victory in one of the Servile Wars. *Servile* comes from the Latin word *servus* – a slave. The war was a slave rebellion led by Spartacus in 73–71 BC, which Pompey helped crush. Nowadays we think of slavery as a crime, but in the times of Pompey most work was done by slaves, even poor Roman families had slaves, so Pompey's victory over Spartacus made him an even bigger hero in Rome.

Next Pompey was sent to fight pirates who were everywhere in the Mediterranean sea. Pompey got rid of them fast. His main weapon was mercy. His fleet seized pirate ships and towns, but Pompey didn't allow his troops to kill rank-and-file pirates. Only the pirate leaders were killed.
So thousands of pirates left their commanders and came to Pompey begging for mercy and forgiveness. They brought their wives and children with them. They explained that the only reason they murdered and plundered as pirates was because they were poor (hmmm....really?).
They promised never to attack Roman towns again. Pompey laughed at their explanations, but accepted their apologies, and let them go. He also gave pirates land that was uninhabited, turning them into farmers. This was celebrated with another amazing triumph in Rome!
"How happy would it have been for him," says Roman historian Plutarch, "if he had ended his life at this point, up to which he enjoyed all that good fortune!"
Pompey won even more military victories, but now he was also fighting for power with other Roman generals. Pompey was good at war, but not a great politician. His main rival, Julius Caesar, was growing more and more powerful. Pompey both admired and feared him.

Fighting to win new lands for the Roman Republic, Caesar defeated many barbarian tribes in Gaul. Gaul, or *Gallia* in Latin, was the area of present-day France in Western Europe. The word *barbarian* comes from the Greek word *barbaros* – foreign. 'Bar...bar' – that's how foreign languages sounded to a Greek ear – like gibberish, and that's how the word *barbaros* was made.

'Barbarian chief Vercingetorix surrenders to Caesar' by Henri-Paul Motte

While fighting in Gaul, says Plutarch, Caesar sent back to Rome a lot of gold and silver and many treasures captured during the wars. He bribed officials in Rome with all that wealth and won them to his side.

In 59 BC Caesar, Pompey, and another Roman general, Crassus, made an agreement called the **First Triumvirate**. **Triumvirate** comes from two Latin words *tres* – three, and *vir* – man. These three men agreed to rule Rome together. But six years later Crassus perished in a battle, while Pompey and Caesar became enemies. Pompey started gathering an army against Caesar. Caesar was ready for a battle. He led his army from Gaul across the Rubicon River toward Rome, and a Civil War broke out. The phrase **he has crossed the Rubicon** became a symbol of 'the point of no return,' meaning 'an action that cannot be undone.' This phrase is still used today, more than 2000 years later!

Caesar's army defeated Pompey. Caesar didn't punish those who had joined Pompey, so many of Pompey's troops and officers switched sides and joined Caesar. When Caesar's troops captured Pompey's camp, says Plutarch, they saw that it didn't look like a military camp, but more like a vacation resort! Every tent was decorated with wreaths of green branches and flowers. There were comfortable couches, and tables loaded with food and wine. Pompey had "a foolish confidence that he would never lose a battle," says Plutarch.

Pompey escaped with only a few followers. No one chased him, so he went quietly away, thinking sad thoughts. Plutarch writes: "For 34 years years Pompey had won every war, and now for the first time, in his old age, he experienced defeat and flight. He thought how in a single hour he had lost all the power and glory he had gained through so many victories."

Pompey took a ship to Egypt. The king of Egypt, Ptolemy, was only 13, and Egypt was ruled mostly by his advisors. Ptolemy's advisors wanted to be friends with Caesar. They invited Pompey to leave his ship, and the moment he reached the shore, he was killed.

'Assassination of Pompey' by Enrico Bandini

They sent Pompey's head and his ring to Caesar. But Caesar never wanted Pompey to be killed. He was shocked when he heard the news, and when he saw the ring, "he burst into tears," says Plutarch. The ring was Pompey's seal. Cut from a gem, it had a lion holding a sword in his paws. Caesar ordered Ptolemey's advisors put to death. Then he defeated Ptolemy's army and put Ptolemy's sister Cleopatra on the throne as the Queen of Egypt.

Julius Caesar

'The head of Pompey' by Giovanni Antonio Pellegrini

Ancient Roman cornelian seal ring with a lion

'Cleopatra' by Frederick Arthur Bridgman

Spartacus was from Thrace, an area around the Black Sea. Plutarch says that his people were nomadic, which means they didn't build villages or towns – instead, they traveled from place to place, living in tents. As a young man Spartacus became a mercenary and joined the Roman army. Mercenaries were soldiers from foreign lands who were paid to be soldiers in the Roman army. However, things didn't work out well for Spartacus. He deserted, that is he ran away from the army. And it was during a war. Spartacus was caught and sold into slavery. He became a *gladiator*.

Gladiators were slaves, trained in a special gladiator school and forced to fight and kill one another in front of thousands of people in Roman theaters. The word gladiator comes from the Latin *gladius,* a broad straight sword about 18 inches (45cm) long. Gladiators fought wild animals and each other, and, since many fights were to the death, sooner or later gladiators perished. When a gladiator was about to lose he had the right to ask for mercy. The crowd then voted whether the loser would live or be killed. Spectators voted for a kill with a *pollice verso*, or 'turned thumb' – similar to our thumb-down gesture. If they wanted the life of the gladiator spared, they raised a fist, hiding the thumb inside the fist – *pollice compresso* – 'compressed thumb.'

'Pollice Verso' by Jean-Léon Gérôme

Roman historian Titus Livy says that when Spartacus was sold into slavery in Rome, he was married to a woman from Thrace. She followed him to the gladiator school. One night when Spartacus went to sleep, a snake crawled into his bed, coiled around his head, but didn't bite him. It stayed on Spartacus' head as he slept, and then left. Spartacus' wife said the snake was a sign from the gods that her husband would gain great power... a terrible power that would end in misfortune.

In 73 BC Spartacus led 70 gladiators to escape from the gladiator school. Titus Livy says that his wife followed the gladiators in their escape. They fought their way out of the building using kitchen knives. Outside there were wagons loaded with weapons and armor for gladiators. The rebels armed themselves and defeated the soldiers who were sent to capture them. Then they went from village to village getting more and more slaves to join them, and plundering the homes of Roman citizens. Their army was small, but they had nothing to lose. They camped on the slopes of Mount Vesuvius, the famous volcano near the city of Pompeii.

At that point the territories of the Roman Republic spread from present-day Spain and France to Greece and the North African coast. Roman provinces paid heavy taxes to Rome and there were endless rebellions that the Roman army was sent to fight. The Roman Senate didn't have even a single legion close to home that they could send to fight Spartacus and his men. Finally, Rome sent a force of only 3,000 men who chased Spartacus higher up Mount Vesuvius. There was only one narrow path leading uphill. The Romans guarded it. On every other side of Vesuvius there were rock cliffs. Spartacus was trapped. The Romans thought they could wait: Spartacus and his men were sure to get hungry and surrender. But Spartacus had a better idea. The gladiators made ropes from the wild vines growing on the slopes of the volcano. They twisted those ropes into ladders, climbed down the cliff face of Vesuvius, went around and behind the Romans, and killed most of the Roman force in a surprise attack.

Rome sent another army, twice as large – 6,000 soldiers. Spartacus and the slaves defeated them and captured all their weapons and armor.

More and more slaves joined Spartacus, and soon his forces grew to over 70,000 men. The gladiators, who were skilled fighters, trained the slaves how to fight. Spartacus' army took a number of towns. The slaves, who were mostly foreigners, hated all Romans. They did not hesitate to rob Roman homes and farms whenever they needed food, horses, or any supplies. Spartacus saw that his army behaved like a mob of criminals, and the people hated them.

Roman gladius

With the whole country against him, he knew that his defeat was only a matter of time. He decided to leave Italy. He hoped to lead his army to the north of Italy, cross the Alps, and over there, in Gaul, dismiss his army, so the former slaves could all go home to their own lands. Meanwhile the Romans managed to gather an army of 8 legions, and were looking for a commander to lead them against Spartacus. None of the Roman generals wanted to face Spartacus' army. The only man who stepped forward was Marcus Licinius Crassus who at that time was the wealthiest Roman citizen. Soon he was joined by Pompey who had just returned with his legions from Spain.

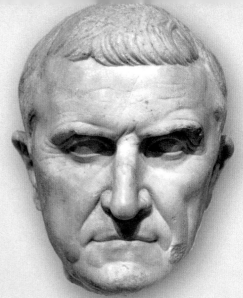

Marcus Licinius Crassus

Crassus pushed Spartacus and the slaves to the south of Italy. Spartacus decided to take his army to the island of Sicily and start a slave uprising over there. To sail to Sicily, he made a deal with Sicilian pirates to use their ships. That was a mistake. The pirates took his money, and sailed away leaving Spartacus to fight the armies of Crassus and Pompey. In 71 BC the forces of Crassus and Pompey attacked. Spartacus was defeated and died in battle.

'Ave Caesar! Morituri te salutant'
(Hail, Caesar, those who are about to die salute you)
by Jean-Léon Gérôme

JULIUS CAESAR

100 – 44 BC

Gaius Julius Caesar was born to a patrician family that was well-known but not wealthy. When he was 16 his father died. Caesar became the head of the family. He took care of his mother Aurelia and his sister Julia, and got married at the age of 17. Around that time Roman general Sulla defeated his enemies, captured Rome and became the Roman dictator. Sulla was an enemy of Caesar's family. He *confiscated* (took away) Caesar's inheritance, and pressed him to divorce his wife Cornelia, whose family also opposed Sulla. Caesar refused to divorce Cornelia, but joined the army and left Rome.

When Sulla died, Caesar returned to Rome as a military hero. He bought a small house for his family, and made his living working as a lawyer. He was also elected to the Roman Senate. When Caesar was 25, he went to Greece to study the art of rhetoric, but his ship was captured by pirates. Caesar was taken captive and locked up at the pirate base on a remote island. The pirates ran a *ransom* business, capturing Romans and demanding that the Roman government pay the ransom. The ransom for a senator was 20 *talents* of gold. A talent was a measure of weight. Caesar told the pirates that 20 talents was not enough, they should ask for 50! The pirates were very surprised, but they went ahead and asked for 50 talents. Caesar waited for ransom for 38 days. All that time he kept busy working on his speech-making skills. He wrote

Roman floor mosaic, 80 BC

poetry and speeches, and read them to the pirates who were guarding him. Plutarch says that if the pirates didn't admire and praise his speeches Caesar called them 'illiterate barbarians' right to their face, and threatened to execute them one day. The pirates laughed at him. After his ransom was paid and he was set free, Caesar sailed to Miletus and gathered there a military force to fight the pirates. Then he returned to the island where he had been kept as a prisoner, captured the pirates and their treasures, and sent both men and gold to the city of Miletus. The ransom was repaid and all the pirates were executed.

At the age of 40 Caesar was elected a consul. Soon he invited Marcus Crassus and Pompey the Great to join him in the First Triumvirate. Between the three of them they had enough money and troops to rule the Roman republic the way they wanted. In order to gain the support of the plebeians, the Triumvirate issued a law that gave a lot of public land - land that belonged to the government - to the poor. Patricians tried to stop the law, but Pompey filled Rome with his soldiers, and scared the enemies of the Triumvirate.

Then Caesar left Rome again: He became the governor of the Roman province of Gaul and a commander of four Roman legions. Soon he conquered all of Gaul and launched an invasion of Britain. "They say that he was led to invade Britain by the hope of getting pearls," writes Suetonius, "and that in comparing their size he sometimes weighed them with his own hand. He was a great collector of gems, carvings, statues, and pictures by ancient artists."

While in Gaul, Caesar wrote a book, *The Gallic Wars*, where he describes battles and negotiations with Germanic and Celtic tribes of Western Europe who opposed the Roman conquest.

'Barbarian chieftan Vercingetorix throws down his arms
at the feet of Julius Caesar' by Lionel Royer

The Gallic Wars is written in the 3rd person. Instead of saying "I ordered my soldiers to build a bridge," it says, "Caesar ordered his soldiers to build a bridge." Caesar's goal was to make his book sound more important and objective. His writing style was very simple and clear, because the book was intended for reading aloud. He sent it chapter by chapter to Rome where it was publicly read on the Forum, increasing his fame and popularity. To get more support from common people, Caesar told many stories of his soldiers' courage and cleverness.

While Caesar was away, Marcus Crassus died in a battle, and Pompey refused to share power with Caesar. The Senate ordered Caesar to give up his military command, and return to Rome to face accusations of corruption in the court of law. That was the end of the First Triumvirate and the beginning of the Roman Civil War. Caesar asked his best legion, *Legio XIII Gemina* (13th Twin Legion), to stay loyal to him even if he disobeyed the orders of the Roman Senate.

Legionaries, or soldiers of the legion, were all professional military men. Usually legionaries served for 25 years, and at the end of their service they were given farm land in Italy. During their service legionaries not only fought the wars, but also did construction work, building roads, bridges, and city walls. Legionaries served mostly far from Rome, in Roman provinces, and were more loyal to their officers and commanders than to the Roman Senate. They admired and respected Caesar.

"He was highly skilled in arms and horsemanship, and had incredible powers of endurance," writes Suetonius. "On the march he always headed his army, sometimes on horseback, but more often on foot, bareheaded both in the heat of the sun and in rain." When his soldiers were scared by a stronger enemy and tried to retreat, Caesar stopped them one by one, and personally led them to face the enemy. Caesar addressed his troops not as *soldiers*, but as *comrades*, and gave them swords and shields decorated with silver and gold.

Once leading an attack on a bridge together with a few of his soldiers, Caesar fell into the water. While his soldiers were all trying to climb into a small boat, Caesar swam a long distance to one of his ships. While swimming, "he was holding up his left hand all the way," says Suetonius, "so as not to wet some papers he was carrying, and dragging his cloak after him with his teeth, to keep the enemy from getting it as a trophy."

With Legio XIII Gemina, Caesar crossed the Rubicon River that was the border of his province, and marched into Italy. Roman historian Suetonius writes that while standing by the Rubicon Caesar said: "Once we cross this little bridge, everything will be decided by the sword." Other historians write that his words were *Alea iacta est* – Let the die be cast.

Plutarch tells us that when Caesar was crossing the Alps his officers pointed at a little mountain village nearby and joked that even in that poor village there was also probably a struggle for power going on, just like in Rome. Hearing that, Caesar said to them, "I would rather be first here than second in Rome."

Hearing that Caesar's legion was headed for Rome, Pompey and most of the Roman Senate left the city in fear. After 18 months of chasing each other, Pompey and Caesar fought the battle of Pharsalus in Greece, and Pompey was defeated. The Senate made Caesar the Dictator of Rome. Unlike Pompey, Caesar didn't kill or banish his political enemies. Anyone who had fought on the side of Pompey was pardoned. According to Suetonius, at the battle of Pharsalus Caesar told his soldiers, "Spare your fellow citizens." And when he saw that the statues of Pompey were thrown down, he ordered to set them up again, since Pompey remained a hero of Rome, even though he was Caesar's enemy.

Caesar celebrated his victories with triumphs and *Triumphal Games*. Roman *games* combined sports events and circus shows, such as chariot races, gladiator fights, and wild animal hunts.

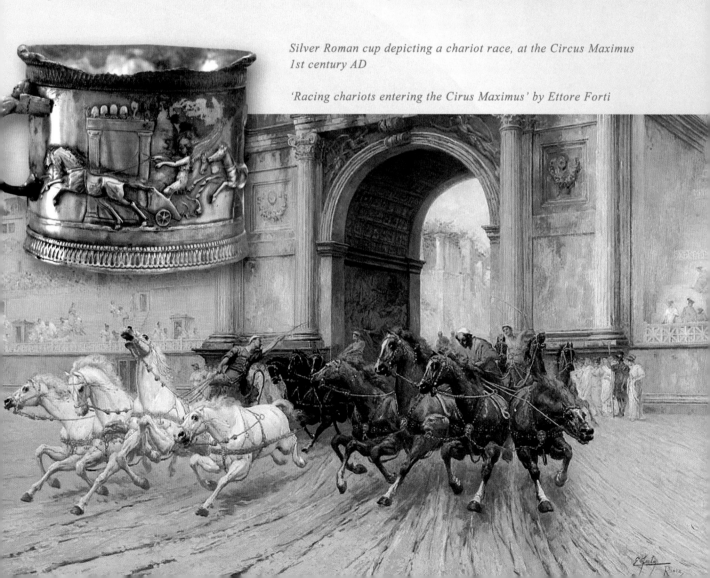

Silver Roman cup depicting a chariot race, at the Circus Maximus 1st century AD

'Racing chariots entering the Cirus Maximus' by Ettore Forti

The games were held in huge arenas and were paid for by wealthy politicians in order to gain popularity with the people. Because most work in Rome was done by slaves who were foreigners captured in wars, a lot of Roman citizens were unemployed and bored. To win elections, Roman politicians used the method of **bread and circuses**: They gave free grain to the poor and staged grand shows that lasted for days.

As part of Caesar's games, 400 lions were hunted and killed in the arena of the great circus in Rome. They held a pretend sea battle, and had two gladiator armies – each 2000 men, 200 horses, and 20 elephants. The gladiators were prisoners of war and they fought to the death in the Roman stadium. In the triumph celebrating his fast victory over the king of Pontus, Caesar's soldiers carried a banner with three words: *Veni, vidi, vici* – 'I came, I saw, I conquered,' in Latin.

Caesar gained more and more power by increasing his authority while decreasing the authority of the Senate. Many laws he issued were very popular with the Roman people. For example, one of his laws forgave almost a quarter of all debts owed by Roman citizens, and another one rewarded families for having many children, since so many people had perished in the wars. He gave farm land to 15 thousand Roman war veterans.

Caesar also changed the calendar! The old Roman calendar was based on the movement of the moon. In 45 BC Caesar replaced it with a calendar based on the sun – the *Julian Calendar*, named after Julius Caesar. It was almost exactly the same as the calendar we use today. Caesar set the length of the year to 365.25 days, and added a leap day at the end of February every fourth year. The Senate named the month of July in honor of Julius Caesar.

Caesar had a bald spot on top of his head, and his enemies made fun of it. "This troubled him greatly," says Suetonius. "He used to comb his hair forward to cover the bald spot, and of all the honors given to him by the senate he made most use of the laurel wreath which he wore at all times to cover his baldness." But when it came to fashion, Caesar liked to be different and didn't care who said what. His senator's tunic had fringed sleeves reaching to the wrist, says Suetonius, which was unheard of before Caesar did it.

Caesar didn't have a son who could inherit his name and his wealth. In this situation Romans often adopted an heir, usually a grownup man who was either a family member or a family friend. Caesar made a will in which he adopted his grandnephew Gaius Octavian (later known as Caesar Augustus) as his son. Octavian was to inherit Caesar's property and bear his name. In case Octavian died before him, Caesar wrote that a young family friend, Decimus Brutus, should be his heir.

Many of Caesar's supporters wanted to crown him king. At a public ceremony where Caesar was sitting on a golden throne, one of his friends, Mark Antony, brought with him a golden crown, and held it out for Caesar to accept. Some people in the crowd started clapping.

But when Caesar pushed the crown away, the whole crowd applauded even louder. Roman historian Cassius Dio says that next Mark Antony saluted Caesar as a king and, putting the crown on Caesar's head, said: "The people offer this to you." But Caesar answered: "Jupiter alone is king of the Romans," and sent the crown to the temple of the god Jupiter. He also asked that it should be recorded in government documents that he had refused to accept the kingship when offered to him by the people through consul Mark Antony. The crown was taken away, but later gold crowns appeared on statues of Caesar in the Forum!

Many people believed that sooner or later Caesar would accept the role of king, and bring an end to the Roman Republic.

Their suspicions seemed to be coming true. In February of 44 BC Caesar accepted being appointed dictator for life. But at that point he had only one month left to live. More than 60 senators made a plot to kill Caesar and restore the powers of the Senate. They called themselves *the Liberators*. On March 15, which the Romans called the *Ides of March*, Caesar was to be present at the Senate. There was a fortune teller, who warned Caesar to be on guard against a great danger on the Ides of march. On March 15, on his way to the Senate Caesar saw the fortune teller and said: "Well, the Ides of March are come!"

The fortune teller responded: "Yes, they are come, but they are not gone."

'Murder of Caesar' by Karl Theodor von Piloty

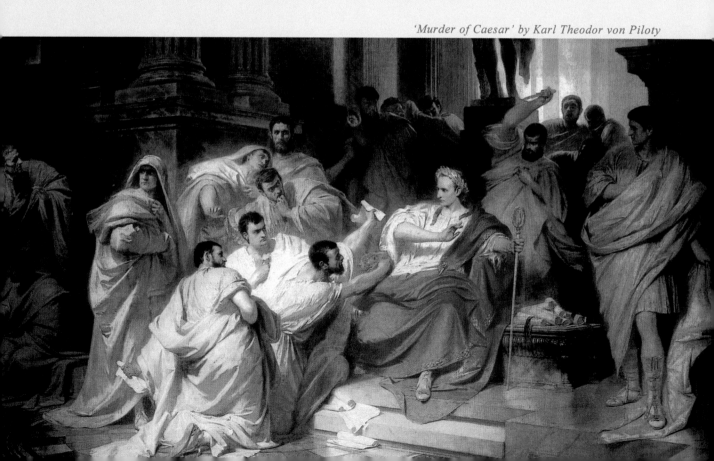

Mark Antony learned about the plot and hurried to the Senate to let Caesar know, but the conspirators managed to stop him. At the Senate the Liberators pulled out their daggers, and attacked Caesar. First, he tried to defend himself, but then, suddenly, he saw a dagger in the hand of Decimus Brutus whom he had adopted as one of his heirs. Caesar's last words were:

Et tu, Brutus? -– "And you, Brutus?" or "You too, Brutus?" He stopped fighting, covered his head with his toga and fell dead on the floor by a pedestal bearing a statue of Pompey.

Soon after Caesar's death he was *deified* – declared to be a god. A comet appeared and was visible for a few days in the evening sky. Romans interpreted it to mean that Caesar had become immortal, writes Cassius Dio, and had taken his place among the stars.

Caesar's family traced their origin to Aeneas, a Trojan warrior and the son of the goddess Venus, so Octavian set up a bronze statue of Caesar in the Temple of Venus in Rome with a star above his head.

CICERO

106 – 43 BC

Marcus Tullius Cicero grew up in an educated and wealthy plebeian family. He studied both Latin and Greek literature and philosophy as a child. When he grew up he studied Roman law and *rhetoric*. In Greek and Latin, the word *rhetoric* means 'the art of speech-making,' or 'the art of persuasion.' Cicero became Rome's most famous *orator*. The Latin word *orator* means a public speaker, someone who makes speeches as part of his profession.

Cicero decided to become a politician. There were strict rules about serving in the government of the Roman Republic.

You had to start your career with 10 years of military service. After that you could get elected to your first government position, but only if you were at least 30 years old. As a government official you were allowed to wear a special toga called a *toga praetexta*.

In ancient Rome, when a boy grew up, the first toga he wore was called *toga virilis* – or a man's toga. It signaled that he was to be treated as an adult and could start his own household, get married and vote in elections. The *toga praetexta* – or 'toga with a border' – worn by government officials, had a purple border. The wider the border, the higher was the government position of the person who wore the toga. The highest government officials wore a *toga picta* – or 'colored toga' – that was all purple and embroidered with gold. Roman purple dye was between purple and a dark red color, close to what we call 'burgundy.' It was the most expensive dye in those days. It was made from sea snails and it took many thousands of snails to produce a small amount of purple dye.

The shell of Murex sea snail used to produce the 'royal purple' dye of ancient Rome

Cicero completed his military service and was elected to serve in the government. He also worked as a lawyer, and became famous for his speeches in court, as he defended citizens who suffered injustice, or proved the corruption of government officials. He lived near the Roman Forum, so that people who wanted his legal advice didn't have to travel far.

Plutarch says that Cicero memorized the names of all the officials and important people in Rome, and also the exact places where they lived in the city and even where their vacation homes were located in the countryside! In Rome most people lived in apartments called *insulae* – islands – in buildings that reached 10 stories high. Wealthy citizens had their own single-family city house (*domus* in Latin), plus a country house, or *villa*. The city houses and apartments were small, but the villas usually had many rooms, pools, exercise rooms, gardens, running water, and even heated floors. A *villa urbana* was a villa that was close to Rome, while a *villa rustica* was a villa that was far in the countryside.

Cicero remembered not only where everyone lived, but also the names of their family members, friends, and neighbors. Cicero's knowledge of their lives made all the leaders feel that Cicero cared about them and their families. This made Cicero very popular.

In 63 BC, Cicero was elected a consul and stopped a plot to overthrow the Roman republic known as the Catiline Conspiracy. The Senate gave him the title *Pater Patria* – Father of the Fatherland. "At this time Cicero had the greatest power in the state," writes Plutarch, "but he made people hate him because he endlessly praised himself... He even went so far as to fill his books and writings with these praises of himself, and because of all that self-praising his speeches became boring and annoying."

'Cicero in the Senate Accusing Catiline of Conspiracy' by Cesare Maccari

Cicero supported Pompey, and feared Caesar. "He was the first to see beneath the surface of Caesar's public policy and to fear it," says Plutarch, "as one might fear the calm surface of the sea, knowing what power is hidden beneath all that kindness and those smiles..." Caesar's political plan was to become a tyrant, thought Cicero. "On the other hand," he wrote in one of his letters, "when I look at Caesar and notice how nicely his hair is brushed, and see him scratching his head with one finger, I cannot think of this man as a criminal who would overthrow the Roman constitution." While Caesar was supported by the plebeians, Cicero was firmly on the side of the aristocracy, the patricians of Rome.

Caesar was generous to his enemies, and respected Cicero. In 60 BC, he asked Cicero to join the First Triumvirate – Caesar, Pompey, and Crassus – in dividing the power in Rome, but Cicero refused. Caesar's supporters felt that Cicero had openly turned against Caesar. They threatened him with exile, and threw stones at him in the street. The Senate voted that the Romans should refuse Cicero fire and water and that no man should give him shelter within five hundred miles of Italy. Cicero grew out his hair, and dressed in black, like he was going to a funeral.

Men of ancient Rome wore their hair short. Few men wore beards: They would not admit you into the Senate unless you shaved. Long hair was a sign of mourning. Black or torn clothes were worn not only as a sign of sadness. Many people wore them in court as a request for pity and understanding.

Finally Cicero felt cornered by Caesar's supporters. He didn't want to leave Rome, and decided to ask Caesar himself for help. When Caesar was returning from a military campaign, Cicero went to meet him outside Rome. He was prepared to be humiliated. But Caesar was as nice and respectful as ever. He got off his horse, hugged Cicero, and walked with him on foot the rest of the way, talking. Caesar "showed him honor and kindness," writes Plutarch. However, when asked for help, Caesar said he was sorry for his supporters' behavior, but there was nothing he could do for Cicero.

Cicero had to leave Rome and go into exile. Far from Rome, he spent time writing books and letters to his friends. "If you have a garden and a library, you have everything you need," he wrote. While he was away, Cicero's house in Rome was seized by the state and demolished. Fortunately, he was allowed to return a year later, and, having learned his lesson, Cicero changed his ways: He began praising Caesar in his speeches and supporting Caesar's ideas.

When the civil war between Caesar and Pompey began, Cicero, again, took Pompey's side. And Caesar was, again, generous: After he won the war, Caesar pardoned Cicero.

'Caesar's funeral' by Prospero Piatti

Despite Caesar's generosity, Cicero had nothing but hatred for him. When Caesar was killed in 44 BC
Cicero was disappointed that the conspirators hadn't invited him to participate in their plot against
Caesar. With Caesar out of the way, Cicero's star was rising again. He took control of the Senate
and tried to undo the damage done by Caesar's dictatorship. He hoped to save the Roman Republic.
Meanwhile, Caesar's adopted son Octavian continued Caesar's work, and needed Cicero's support.
Plutarch says that Octavian admired Cicero and even called him 'father.' But Cicero ignored him.
He thought Octavian, who was only 19 years old, was too young and inexperienced to become a real
force in Roman politics. I would "praise, raise, and erase" Octavian, he boasted. He was wrong.
Octavian was to end the Roman Republic and become Caesar Augustus, the first emperor of Rome.
To Cicero's surprise, in no time Octavian joined forces with Mark Antony and the Roman general
Lepidus to form the **Second Triumvirate**. They seized power in Rome and sent their troops to chase
and kill the enemies of Caesar. Mark Antony demanded that Cicero's name be added to the list of
the enemies to be killed first. Octavian disagreed. He argued with Mark Antony for two days, trying
to save Cicero, but then he gave up. Cicero was proclaimed an enemy of the state. As soldiers hunted
him, many Romans who still admired Cicero helped him hide, but soon he was found and killed.

Many years later, after he became an Emperor, Octavian came to see one of his grandsons. "He found
the boy reading a book by Cicero!" writes Plutarch. Scared, the boy tried to hide the book under his
clothes, but Octavian saw it. He took the book, and stood there, silently, reading it. Then he gave the
book back to his grandson with these words: "Cicero was a learned man, my child, and he loved his
country." As generous as Caesar, Octavian also helped Cicero's son to become a consul.

MARK ANTONY

83 – 30 BC

Mark Antony was one of Caesar's generals. During the Gallic Wars he was a legate and commanded two legions. As the First Triumvirate fell apart, Mark Antony took Caesar's side and crossed the Rubicon River with him to start the Civil War against Pompey.

Antony was very popular with his soldiers. He liked to tell them stories of his adventures, and joked about his girlfriends. He often chose to eat with the common soldiers, sitting at their tables instead of with his officers. This was very unusual for a Roman commander.

Marc Antony also held endless parties and celebrations. Unlike Caesar who lived in a simple tent and often slept on the ground during military campaigns, Marc Antony insisted on the most elegant and expensive lifestyle. His wine was brought to him in golden cups. Dinnertime saw him relaxing on fancy carpets, always placed where he could enjoy his meal while also enjoying a spectacular view. One time he even had his chariot drawn by lions!

His wife Fulvia was not interested in women's work like sewing or housekeeping, says Plutarch. "She wished to rule a ruler and command a commander," and Mark Antony obeyed her orders.

'Mark Anthony makes a speech after Caesar's death' by George Edward Robertson

After Caesar was killed, Caesar's wife, Calpurnia, sent gold and other treasures from Caesar's house to Marc Antony for safekeeping. But when Caesar's adopted son Octavian came to Rome and claimed Caesar's property, Antony didn't want to give back the treasures. Octavian, of course, insisted. In his will, Caesar had directed Octavian to give every Roman a gift of seventy-five drachmas from Caesar's money. But Antony despised Octavian, treated him like a kid, and told him he was crazy to give away Caesar's fortune. "When Octavian refused to listen to this, and demanded the money, Antony kept saying and doing many things to insult him," says Plutarch. Finally Octavian encouraged Antony's enemy Cicero to attack Antony in his speeches. At that moment Cicero controlled the Senate and was very powerful. The Senate declared Antony an enemy of the state. Antony agreed to return Caesar's money, and had to leave Rome.

He went north with his legions, and had to cross the Alps with no food or supplies. "But it was Antony's nature to rise to his highest level when he faced difficulties," writes Plutarch. "He was an amazing example to his soldiers." He drank water from dirty streams, ate wild fruit, tree bark, and roots with his soldiers and never complained.
Mark Antony hoped that since he was so popular with the troops, Caesar's legions would stay loyal to him, but he was mistaken. Two whole legions left Antony and asked Octavian to be their commander. Octavian was too young to be a military commander. He was just a private citizen, but Caesar's soldiers didn't care. As Cicero said in one of his speeches,
"In times of war, the law falls silent."

In August of 43 BC Octavian marched on Rome with eight legions and took control of the city. To prevent a new civil war, Octavian, Antony, and the Roman General Lepidus formed the *Second Triumvirate* – an agreement to divide power and split control over the provinces of the Roman Republic between them. The Triumvirate declared the Liberators, Caesar's murderers and their supporters, enemies of the state. One third of the Roman Senate, including Cicero, was executed. The armies of the Liberators were defeated.

According to the agreement of the Triumvirate, Mark Antony was to rule Rome's eastern provinces, including Egypt. He sent a messenger to Egyptian Queen Cleopatra, and ordered her to come meet him. He suspected treason and wanted to know why she had given some money to the army of the Liberators. "But when Antony's messenger saw how beautiful Cleopatra was," writes Plutarch, "and noticed her cleverness in conversation, he instantly knew that Antony would never do such a woman any harm. He thought that she would have a great influence on Anthony." The messenger convinced Cleopatra to try and win Antony's trust with her beauty and charm.

Cleopatra arrived to meet Antony on a ship with purple sails. It was decorated with gold and its oars were silver. She looked like Venus, the goddess of Love, says Plutarch. Her servants were dressed as **nymphs** – nature spirits. Her musicians played exotic music. The aroma of rare perfumes filled the air. Cleopatra offered Antony a magnificent feast of unusual and delicious foods, and captivated him with her skill in conversation.

Cleopatra was Greek, coming from a line of kings going back to Ptolemy Soter, one of the generals of the Greek conqueror Alexander the Great. She was extremely well-educated and spoke many languages, including Latin, Greek, Egyptian, Hebrew, Syrian, and Arabic. She never needed an interpreter when talking to foreigners, says Plutarch, unlike the kings of Egypt before her who spoke only Greek and had made no effort to learn even Egyptian, the language of the land they ruled.

Antony quickly fell in love with Cleopatra. He left his wife Fulvia and moved to Egypt to live with Cleopatra in her palace at Alexandria.

'THe meeting of Anthony and Cleopatra' by Lawrence Alma Tadema

'Cleopatra' by John William Waterhouse

To keep Antony under her influence, Cleopatra never left him alone. "She played dice with him, partied with him, hunted with him, and watched him as he exercised," writes Plutarch. Sometimes at night they dressed as servants, ran away from Cleopatra's palace and played pranks on people in the streets. A few times Antony got in street fights and came home badly beaten. Many people upset with his pranks suspected who he was, but Egyptians liked him, and everything was forgiven.

Once Antony had bad luck while fishing with Cleopatra. He didn't want her to laugh at him and ordered his fishermen to dive under his boat and secretly attach a fish to his hook. But Cleopatra figured out his trick, and the next day she had her servant dive under the boat and attach a dried and salted herring to Antony's hook.

When Antony pulled it out, everyone laughed at him, and Cleopatra said: "Imperator, leave fishing to fishermen! Your sport is to capture cities, kingdoms, and continents."

Antony and Cleopatra held feasts and parties every day. Philotas, a doctor who was studying medicine in Alexandria, once happened to be in Cleopatra's palace kitchen. He saw 8 wild boars roasting, and so many other dishes being prepared, that he asked how many guests were expected by the Queen. "Oh, it's only Cleopatra, Antony, and a couple guests," answered Cleopatra's chef. "We usually prepare many dinners, because Antony has dinner every day at a different time, and he always wants it fresh and perfect. So we keep making dinners until he asks for dinner." Antony's son, a kid who lived with Anthony and Cleopatra, liked a joke made by Philotas, and decided to reward him. He pointed at a table with a lot of gold cups and dishes, and said, "All this I give to you!" The doctor thought it was a joke, but the servants put the gold items in a sack and handed it to him. As he was leaving, one of the servants said quietly to him, "May I offer you money instead of these treasures? If the boy's father notices that some of these gold things are gone, he will be upset, because these are precious works of ancient art."

Cleopatra

Antony and Cleopatra lived as husband and wife, and had kids, but they were not married. Roman law allowed divorce and remarriage. Though divorcing a husband or a wife of many years was considered a shame, divorces and marriages were used by leading families of Rome to create alliances and share power. Marc Antony wanted to marry Cleopatra, but was afraid that divorcing his wife Fulvia would cause him political problems back in Rome. But soon Fulvia died. Meanwhile, the relationship between Antony and Octavian became shaky. Antony decided to return to Rome to work things out between them. Octavian thought that Cleopatra's influence on Antony was dangerous. Since Fulvia had passed away, Octavian asked Antony to marry Octavian's sister, Octavia. If you marry my sister, this will seal our loyalty to each other, he said. Mark Antony agreed to marry Octavia. Octavia was beautiful, loyal, and loved Antony. For a couple years they lived together in Rome and had kids, but then everything changed. Antony needed troops for a war in Parthia (ancient Iran), but Octavian didn't want to share his legions with Antony. A solution was found by – guess who? – Cleopatra! Egypt had one of the biggest armies in the Eastern Roman provinces. Cleopatra suggested to Antony that they join their armies together to give him victory.

Antony and Cleopatra's combined Roman-Egyptian army was enormous, but as a commander Antony made so many mistakes that the Parthian war was a disaster. Plutarch blamed everything on Cleopatra. "Antony was so eager to spend the winter with her that he began the war before the proper time, and managed it poorly," he writes. "He was not his own master. It almost seemed like he was under a magic spell, thinking only of going back to Cleopatra, not of defeating the enemy."

'The Roman wedding' by Emilio Vasarri

Octavia missed Antony and asked her brother permission to visit him in Greece where he said he would stop with his troops. She raised money and gathered gifts for Antony's officers, as well as clothing and food for his soldiers, and traveled to Athens to meet him. But there she received a letter from Antony telling her that the war was not going well and he was not coming to see her.

Mark Anthony and Octavia on a silver Roman tetradrachm coin, 39 BC

Cleopatra heard that Octavia was trying to reunite with Antony, and decided to prevent this. She traveled to Syria to meet him and pretended she was so in love with him that she would cry the moment he turned away or left the room. Cleopatra's advisors, whom Plutarch calls "flatterers" kept telling Antony that Octavia had married him only because of her brother, but Cleopatra truly loved him. Cleopatra would die from sadness without you, they told Antony. "Finally they melted the man to such an extent that he went back to Alexandria – and Cleopatra," writes Plutarch.

When Octavia returned to Rome from Athens, Octavian was so angry, he didn't want his sister to live in Antony's house. He ordered her and her kids to move to his own house instead. But Octavia realized that her brother was planning to use her to start a civil war against Antony. Octavian's power was growing. It was time for Octavian to get rid of Antony. Octavia refused to leave Antony's house and begged Octavian to change his mind. It would be a shame, she told Octavian, if the two most powerful men in Rome started a civil war because of two women – Octavia and Cleopatra.

Octavia was a woman of loyal and noble character, say Roman historians. She adopted the kids Antony had with his wife Fulvia, and raised them as her own. She also helped Antony's friends if any of them needed anything from Octavian. But Antony didn't appreciate her. While in Alexandria, he announced his divorce from Octavia, and sent messengers to Rome who had orders to eject Octavia from his house. Octavia left it in tears, taking her own and Fulvia's kids with her. Antony's friends thought the divorce was a big mistake, says Plutarch, especially those who had seen Cleopatra and knew that Octavia was far more beautiful, more intelligent, and a kinder person than Cleopatra.

In 32 BC, the Roman Senate declared war against Cleopatra. Addressing the Senate, Octavian said that Antony had been drugged by Cleopatra and was not in control of himself. Cleopatra and Antony were scared and tried to negotiate peace. Octavian ignored Antony, but he sent word to Cleopatra that she would be pardoned if she either killed Antony or threw him out of Egypt.
Cleopatra refused to betray Antony.

Cleopatra on a silver coin

In 31 BC, the war started. The fleet of Antony and Cleopatra was defeated at the Battle of Actium, and Octavian invaded Egypt. Antony kept fighting, but his soldiers were deserting him. At that point they had more respect for Octavian than for Antony. One day, after Antony had successfully fought off Octavian's troops, "he went into the palace," writes Plutarch, "kissed Cleopatra, all armed as he was, and presented to her one of his soldiers who had fought most bravely. Cleopatra gave the man a helmet and armor made of gold as a reward. The man took them, of course, but later that night deserted to Octavian."

Antony challenged Octavian to one-on-one combat, but Octavian responded, "You have many other ways of dying." Then Antony decided to fight one last battle and 'die with honor' in that battle. As he announced this during dinner, he noticed that some of his friends had tears in their eyes. He then changed his mind again, telling them that he would not lead them into battle after all: All he wanted was to die with honor, he said. He knew he wouldn't win.

The next day Antony stabbed himself with a sword and died from the wound. Fearful that she would be paraded in Rome in Octavian's victory triumph, with his sister Octavia present, Cleopatra had a venomous snake brought to her in a basket full of fruit. She let the snake bite her and she died. "In this way, Antony and Cleopatra, who had caused many evils to the Egyptians and many to the Romans, met their death," observed Roman historian Cassius Dio.

'Death of Cleopatra' by Juan Luna

'Roman family and their guests' by Ettore Forti

In his **Roman History** Cassius Dio had some unflattering things to say about both Antony and Cleopatra. Antony had a great heart but the mind of a slave, he wrote. "He would plunder the property of others and waste his own. He showed compassion to many without cause and punished even more without justice... Cleopatra was of insatiable greed and easily swayed by flattery."

In Rome, the Senate took down the statues of Antony and decreed that nobody from the Antony family should ever be named *Mark*. That happened when Cicero's son was serving as a consul. The gods took their vengeance on Antony for Cicero's death, concluded the Romans.

Mark Anthony and Octavian on a Roman aureus coin issued in 41 BC to celebrate the Second Triumvirate

'Road to Pompeii' by Ettore Forti

CAESAR AUGUSTUS

63 BC – 14 AD

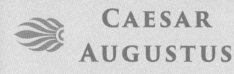

With Mark Antony dead, Octavian became
the ruler of Rome. Suddenly, everyone in Rome
was telling stories about 'signs' that had supposedly
predicted the rise of Octavian. In his *Roman History*
Cassius Dio reports a few of those stories.
"While Octavian lived in the countryside as a child,
an eagle snatched from his hands a loaf of bread and after
soaring high up, it flew down and gave it back to him...
When Octavian was a teenager and was staying in Rome,
Cicero had a dream that a boy had been let down from the sky
by golden chains. The boy arrived on the Capitol square holding
in his hand a whip he had received from the god Jupiter. Cicero
did not know who the boy in his dream was. The next day, on
the Capitol, Cicero met Octavian and realized that Octavian was
the boy in his dream!" Well, by the time Octavian became the Roman
ruler Cicero was long dead, so nobody could ask him if that story was true!

In 27 BC the Senate gave Octavian the title of *Augustus* which means 'majestic.'
He became Caesar Augustus. That night the river Tiber that flows through Rome rose and flooded
a lot of Roman neighborhoods. It's a sign from gods, said the Romans: Octavian Augustus will rise
even higher! The month of August was named after him. All over Rome people were competing
in flattery toward Octavian. One man announced he loved Octavian Augustus so much that
"he was going to make Augustus his heir on equal terms with his own son!" writes Cassius Dio.
"Not that he had much of anything," he adds...

At first Octavian, or Caesar Augustus, did not call himself emperor, instead using the title *Princeps
Civitatis* - First among Citizens. But soon the Senate named him *imperator*, or emperor.
"That's not the title 'Imperator' which had occasionally been given to generals in honor of their
victories," says Cassius Dio, "but rather 'Imperator' in the other use of this word: The one who
holds supreme power." The Senate and the government were still in place, but the emperor
was the final authority.

After the Senate had elected Augustus consul for the 10th time, they "freed him from obeying the laws, in order that he might be a supreme ruler over the laws and do everything he wished and not do anything he did not wish." (Cassius Dio)

"Augustus never made war on any nation without just cause," writes Roman historian Suetonius. "He was so far from desiring to increase his power or military glory at any cost, that he forced the chiefs of barbarian tribes to take an oath in the temple of Mars the Avenger that they would faithfully keep the peace for which they asked... He used to say that you should never start a war unless the hope of gain was clearly greater than the fear of loss." And his favorite sayings were: "More haste, less speed," "Better a safe commander than a bold commander," and "That is done quickly enough which is done well enough."

As a result, Augustus was very successful and respected as a ruler.

The only bad breaks he suffered were two military defeats at the hands of German tribes in Gaul. In one of them three legions led by Quintilius Varus were killed to the last man in the Teutoburg Forest. Upon receiving the news, Augustus Caesar could be heard slamming his head on the palace walls and screaming "Quintilius Varus, give me back my legions!!" He dressed in black on that day every year for the rest of his life.

Augustus was also good at making speeches and persuading people. He had studied literature, history, and rhetorical art since his childhood, and even in time of war he read books and practiced reading poetry aloud every day. As an emperor, he stopped memorizing his speeches and instead started reading them from paper to save time and make sure he didn't forget anything.

He got so used to writing down his thoughts that even in conversations with his wife Livia he prepared notes and read them to her from a notebook. He never gave up learning, and even in old age he took classes in speech writing and public speaking.

'Germanic king Arminius attacks the Romans in the Teutoburg Forest' by Peter Theodor Janssen

Suetonius praises Augustus as a thoughtful man and a caring family member. Rebuilding the Roman Forum Augustus made it narrower than he had planned, because he did not want to bother the owners of the neighbouring houses. When he recommended his sons for government positions, he always added "If they are worthy of it." The only two weaknesses Augustus had, according to Suetonius, were a fear of thunder and lightning, and a hatred of getting up early in the morning.

Whenever a storm began, he hid in an underground room in his palace! And when he had to address the Senate early in the morning he begged to stay at his friends' houses near the Forum so he didn't have to get up too early.

Augustus loved his grandkids and taught them himself, giving them lessons in reading, writing, and swimming. He was proud of his beautiful handwriting, and insisted that his grandkids learn to write as well as he could. He made sure they sat right next to him at dinner, and took them along when traveling. Augustus wore simple clothes made by his sister, wife, daughter or granddaughters, says Suetonius. The purple stripe on his toga was neither narrow, nor broad. The only special item he owned was his shoes. They had thick soles to make him look taller than he really was.

The emperor also came up with a party game, where he sold to his dinner guests mystery items: Some were precious, and others were of no value, but you were not told what each item was. You had to guess. For example, he would sell a painting but show it only from the back. Some guests won real treasures, while others bought things that were useless.

Augustus ruled for 40 years until his death in 14 AD. His last words were, *Have I played the part well? Then applaud as I exit!* After his death, his stepson, Tiberius, became the second emperor of Rome.

Portrait of Livia, AD 4   *'The carpet seller' by Ettore Forti*

VIRGIL

70 – 19 BC

Virgil, or Publius Vergilius Maro, was a Roman poet. Virgil's most famous work, the epic poem *The Aeneid*, remains one of the most impressive masterpieces of Western literature.

Virgil's parents were common Roman citizens living in the countryside. Suetonius says his father was a potter. It is also believed that his family owned some woodlands where they raised honey bees. The day before Virgil was born, his mother had a dream "that she gave birth to a laurel branch, which on touching the earth took root and grew at once to the size of a full-grown tree, covered with fruits and flowers of various kinds." Many Romans trusted in various signs and omens. They believed that these could predict the future. Virgil's mother's dream was one such omen. Suetonius tells a story of another omen predicting the future greatness of Virgil. It was a custom among the Romans to plant a poplar tree when a baby was born. The poplar branch planted by Virgil's parents "grew so fast in a short time that it equalled in size poplars planted long before!"

Virgil started writing poetry when he was 16 years old and soon became well-known for his poetic gift. Wealthy Romans offered him gifts of gold and money in admiration, and Caesar Augustus offered him a house in Rome as a gift. Virgil, however, was shy. He rarely came to Rome and lived mostly in the countryside.

'Aeneas' flight from Troy' by Frederico Barocci

'The meeting of Dido and Aeneas' by Nathaniel Dance-Holland

The Aeneid was written to continue the epic poetry tradition of Homer, the great Greek author of **The Iliad** and **The Odyssey**. Its theme was the origin of the city of Rome. To strengthen his rule, Augustus encouraged writers and artists to create works that glorified the history of Rome and the task of Roman civilization to rule the world. In Virgil's **Aeneid**, Aeneus, the legendary ancestor of Julius Caesar and Caesar Augustus, says: "Roman, remember to use your strength to rule the Earth's peoples!" And Jupiter, the king of the gods himself, promises that Rome will **rule without end**.

The Aeneid is the legend of Aeneas, son of the goddess Venus, who survived the destruction of Troy and founded a city in Italy which would become Rome. Aeneas is mentioned in Homer's poem **The Iliad** as one of the defenders of Troy. In **The Aeneid**, he escapes Troy carrying his old father in his arms. After 6 years of looking for a new home, a storm brings the ships of Aeneas to Carthage. He is welcomed there by queen Dido, who falls in love with him and hopes to marry him. But Jupiter, the king of the gods, sends the messenger god Mercury to Aeneas, reminding him that he must continue his journey and find a new land for his people. Aeneas leaves Carthage secretly, and Dido is so upset she utters a curse, making the cities of Carthage and Rome enemies forever.

Latinus, king of the Latins in Italy, welcomes Aeneas to his land. Aeneas becomes engaged to marry Latinus' daughter Lavinia. But Turnus, king of the Rutuli, who hoped to marry Lavinia, declares war against the Latins. Aeneas wins the war and that's the end of *The Aeneid.*

It is said that Augustus commissioned *The Aeneid* to Virgil, that is, asked him to write it and paid for it. So it's not surprising that Virgil flatters Augustus and praises his great achievements in *The Aeneid*. Virgil worked on *The Aeneid* for 11 years. He first wrote it in prose, and then started rewriting it in poetic verses. Romans couldn't wait to hear each new chapter. When Caesar Augustus was away waging war in one of the Roman provinces, he wrote letters to Virgil begging him to send "something from *The Aeneid*," even just a draft! Virgil was often asked to read *The Aeneid* at parties, and was invited by Augustus to read it to the emperor's family. Suetonius says that Octavia, Augustus' sister, became so emotional listening to Virgil's reading that she fainted!

Virgil finished *The Aeneid*, and decided to spend the following three years polishing and editing it. He didn't want to publish the whole poem without making it absolutely perfect. Unfortunately he soon became very sick, so sick he thought he might die. Virgil asked his friend Varius to burn *The Aeneid* if he died before finishing it. Varius refused. On his deathbed "Virgil constantly called for his book boxes, intending to burn the poem himself," says Suetonius. But his friends kept his writings safe, and after Virgil's death the poem was officially published on Caesar Augustus' request.

'Virgil reading The Aeneid to Caesar Augustus, Octavia, and Livia' by Jean-Baptiste Wicar

CALIGULA

AD 12 – 41

Caligula, or Gaius Julius Caesar Augustus Germanicus was the third
Roman emperor. His mother was Agrippina, a granddaughter of Augustus,
and his dad was the Roman general Germanicus. *Caligula* means
'little boot.' It was a nickname given to him by his dad's soldiers when
he accompanied his father on a military campaign in Germany.

Caligula's mom, Agrippina, hated Tiberius, the second
Roman Emperor, and Caligula's brothers perished in palace
conspiracies against Tiberius. Tiberius was afraid of
conspiracies and preferred to live far from Rome, on the island
of Capri. For some reason he liked Caligula and invited him
to stay with him at his palace on Capri. Six years later
Tiberius died and Caligula became the emperor.

Some Roman historians believed that Tiberius didn't die on his own, but was killed by Caligula
who is thought to have hated Tiberius just as much as his mother and brothers did. Not long before
Tiberius' death, a fortune teller told him that Caligula had "no more chance of becoming emperor
than of riding a horse across the Gulf of Baiae." Caligula learned of this, and after he became
emperor he ordered a group of ships to line up across the Gulf of Baiae to create a floating bridge.
The 'bridge' was over 2 miles long. Caigula rode his favorite horse, Incitatus, from ship to ship
and crossed the gulf!

Romans disliked Tiberius and were happy to see Caligula, the son of the famous general, become
their ruler. Suetonius tells us that at the funeral of Tiberius people were laughing and celebrating,
instead of crying, and when Caligula showed up all dressed in black, they cheered,
calling him *our baby*, *our star*, and even *our little chick*! "Full and absolute power was at once
placed in his hands by unanimous consent of the Senate – and of the crowds," says Suetonius.

Caligula's first acts were very popular. He increased the military men's salaries, reduced taxes,
called the enemies of Tiberius back from exile, and even brought back democratic elections!
Interestingly, many politicians in Rome objected to that. They thought that if people were again
allowed to elect whoever they wanted to the government, the government wouldn't be as good!

"So much for Caligula as emperor," says Suetonius in his Life of Caligula,
"we must now tell of his career as a monster."

Soon after Caligula became an emperor, a disaster struck. The emperor fell sick, and many suspected that he was poisoned. After Caligula recovered from his illness, he seemed to have become a different man. He became suspicious, and started killing or exiling his friends and advisors without any trial. He executed his father-in-law, brother-in-law, and his cousin.

His grandmother was poisoned! He sent his two sisters into exile!

"He was crazy the way he spent money," reports Suetonius. "He would bathe in perfume, drink pearls of great price dissolved in vinegar, and set before his guests bread and meat made of gold, saying 'Either save money, or be an emperor!'" When he led his troops to war, he was so lazy that "he was carried by eight soldiers, and demanded that people from the towns along the road sweep the road for him and sprinkle it with water to get rid of the dust!"

'A Roman feast' by Roberto Bompiani   *Portrait of Caligula on an onyx ring, 37 BC*

It was not surprising that very soon another disaster struck. The Emperor spent all the money of the treasury, and there was nothing left! Caligula asked people to lend him money, and started sending wealthy politicians into exile so he could seize their wealth and pay his debts. Whenever he seized the treasures of his enemies, "he used to throw himself each time on the gold and silver he captured, and roll in it," says Cassius Dio.

He also came up with a new way to make money. He raised taxes, but had his new laws written in very small letters on a tablet which he hung up in a high place, so that no one could really read it. Not knowing the law, people made mistakes paying their taxes, and all their property was taken away as punishment. If they protested, Caligula had his soldiers kill them on the spot.

And, of course, Caligula didn't stop spending money. He started building grand temples, aqueducts, theaters, and enlarged his palace. The aqueducts carried fresh water from lakes or rivers to the cities. The cities had underground pipes and sewage systems. Wealthy homes had running water! Roman Baths were places where people not only bathed, but also socialized, discussed politics, and did business. The floors of the baths were heated by a system that circulated hot air under the floors. Some baths had libraries, reading rooms, gardens, and food service! Caligula brought a giant stone obelisk from Egypt and placed it in the center of Rome. He built a couple of floating palaces. One of them was so huge that it had marble floors and running water!

Some people thought the emperor was crazy. He ordered that the most famous statues of gods be brought to Rome from all over Italy and Greece, then had their heads removed – and replaced with his own head!! His palace grew so large that it swallowed one of the temples on the Forum. Caligula made it an entry hallway of his palace and greeted his guests dressed as the god Jupiter, his beard painted gold, and a golden thunderbolt in his hand! He also built a separate temple for himself. Inside was a life-size pure-gold statue of Caligula which was dressed every day in the same clothes that the emperor wore that day.

"He was not at all respectful towards the Senate," says Suetonius. Senators who needed to talk to the emperor had to run in their togas for several miles beside his chariot and to serve him at his table, standing napkin in hand, like a waiter!"

Once, at a theater where gladiators were supposed to fight wild animals such as lions, there were not enough gladiators. What to do? Caligula was bored. So he ordered his guards to take a bunch of people who came to the theater to watch the show, and throw them into the arena to be killed by the wild beasts.

"He was very tall and extremely pale," says Suetonius, " with an unshapely body, and very thin neck and legs. His hair was thin and entirely gone on the top of his head. Because of this people were not allowed to look at Caligula from any point higher than where he was standing. His body was hairy. If anyone for any reason mentioned a goat, the emperor thought they were laughing at his hairy body, and put them to death. His face was ugly. He learned to make scary faces at himself in the mirror, and then tried to look even uglier by making those faces in public."

Caligula suffered from sleeplessness, sleeping not more than 3 hours a night. And he had all sorts of scary dreams. One night he dreamed that the spirit of the Ocean spoke to him. He was so scared, he got out of bed and wandered around his palace for the rest of the night, like a ghost.

Caligula didn't like people, but he loved his horse Incitatus. If it was noisy outside of his palace, he sent his soldiers to order silence in the neighbourhood, so his horse could sleep. He built for it a stall (a room) of marble, and a manger (a container for horse food like grass or grain) of ivory (elephant tusks). He ordered that when cold, his horse should be covered with purple blankets dyed with the same precious purple dye as a consul's toga picta. His horse wore a collar of precious stones, had expensive furniture in its stall, and lots of slaves to serve it. Caligula also sent party invitations for his friends to come to his horse's parties. At those parties, there was music, poetry readings for his horse, and all guests had to come dressed in their most elegant clothes.

Finally, Caligula had so little respect for the Senate, that he came up with the idea of making his horse a consul, which was the highest position in the Senate.

When that failed, he made the horse a priest.

'Chariot race winner' by Ettore Forti

'Claudius hiding behind the curtains' by Laurence Alma Tadema

In AD 41 Caigula's guards and a few senators plotted to murder the emperor. Their plan was successful. They surrounded Caligula in the underground passage at his palace, stabbed him to death, and started looking for his family members. They killed Caligula's wife and their daughter, but his uncle, Claudius, hid behind the palace window curtains and survived. He became the fourth emperor of Rome.

During the reign of Claudius the Romans founded the city of Londinium in the province of Britain. It later became London. The Romans built a network of roads throughout England and defensive walls to keep barbarians outside of the borders of the empire.

Roman baths in the city of Bath, England

NERO

AD 37 – 68

Nero Claudius Caesar Augustus Germanicus was the
5th Roman emperor. His mother Agrippina was a sister of
Emperor Caligula. When Nero's father died, emperor Claudius
married Agrippina, so Nero became the stepson of Claudius.

Claudius already had a son, Britannicus, but Agrippina wanted
her son Nero to be the next emperor. So she convinced Claudius
to name Nero the heir to the throne. Nero's private teacher was
Seneca, the famous Roman philosopher. He taught Nero literature
and history, but Nero's mother, Agrippina, didn't allow her son
to study philosophy. It's not helpful for a future ruler,
she warned him. "Seneca tutored Nero in public speaking
and was a man of decency and friendly attitude," writes Roman historian Tacitus.

When emperor Claudius died in 54 AD, there were rumors that Nero's mother poisoned Claudius.
Despite that, Nero was crowned Emperor of Rome. He was 17.

In the early days of his reign Nero was popular. Like Cicero, he remembered everyone's name and
was very friendly. When he was asked to sign a death sentence, he said, "How I wish I had never
learned to write!" Seneca became his advisor, and kept him from making many dreadful mistakes.
But soon Nero stopped following Seneca's advice and his behavior became more and more bizarre.
"He was carried away by a craze for popularity," explains Suetonius, "and he was jealous of
anyone who people liked. He had a longing for immortality and undying fame."

Nero loved reading his own poems and singing at the theater. He imagined he was a great actor
and singer. "While he was singing no one was allowed to leave the theatre for any reason,"
wrote Suetonius. "Many people were worn out by listening to him and applauding him for hours.
Some escaped by jumping down from the theater wall, because the gates were locked.
Others pretended they had died and were carried out of the theater to be buried."
Nero watched carefully how his friends applauded him: Those who applauded loudly and for
a long time were rewarded, and those who didn't applaud long enough were treated like enemies.
Nero also appointed five thousand soldiers to lead the applause at the theater, just in case it was
not loud enough.

"On one occasion after holding a wild-beast hunt at the theater," says Cassius Dio, "Nero ordered the theater flooded with water to hold a sea fighting demonstration. Then he let the water out again and called in the gladiators to fight. Last of all, he flooded the place once more and served a feast... In the centre of the lake they floated empty wooden barrels, and on top of these was placed a wooden floor... Nero and his friends sat in the center of the floating platform on purple rugs and soft cushions, while all the rest made merry around them."

"As the evening came, Nero would conceal himself with a cap or a wig," says Suetonius," and wander in the streets playing pranks on people. Those pranks were far from harmless. He used to beat up people returning home from late dinner parties, and if they resisted, he stabbed them to death and threw them into the sewers. He would even break into shops and rob them! He set up a market in his palace, where he sold things he stole."

Nero's mother, Agrippina, wanted to rule through her son. She didn't tolerate any competition and murdered anyone who had any influence on Nero. "Agrippina was burning with the desire to use her criminally-gained power," says Tacitus. "In the closets of his palace Nero found some dresses and other things which had been worn in the past by previous wives and mothers of emperors. He selected the most beautiful dress and jewellery, and sent them as a gift to his mother... Agrippina, however, loudly declared that the dress he had sent her was worse than her own clothes, and that her ungrateful son had stolen all the treasures..."

'Gladiator sea battle' by Ulpiano Checa

Agrippina

Nero learned from his mother. His stepbrother Britannicus turned 14. To threaten Nero, Agrippina praised Britannicus saying that now that he had grown up, he could be emperor too. Right away, Nero had Britannicus poisoned. Here is how Tacitus describes the poisoning of Britannicus: "Britannicus' food and drink were always tasted by a servant to prevent poisoning, so the murderers came up with a special clever plot. They served the boy a drink which was harmless, but very hot. The servant tasted it and passed it to Britannicus, but Britannicus rejected it because it was too hot. Then they poured in some cold water, and that water was poisoned. Suddenly, Britannicus fell silent and stopped breathing. Everyone sitting around froze in fear. Some, not knowing what had just happened, ran away looking for help. Those, who did understand, sat still, staring at Nero. But he said that this was not unusual. He added that Britannicus was just sick. Agrippina gave a momentary glimpse of her terror and distress, even though she tried to control her expression and hide it. But it was clear from this that she had known nothing about this and neither had Octavia, Nero's wife and Britannicus's own sister."

Agrippina's control over Nero was weakening, and soon Nero had his mother killed as well. He invited Agrippina to join him at a festival in Baiae, and when she was about to leave, he gave her a gift, a beautiful boat with a crew. The boat was a death trap.

'Roman empress embarking on a boat' by Ettore Forti

Cameo with a portrait of Nero, AD 20   *'Nero ordering the murder of his mother' by N.Coypel*

On her way home on the boat, Nero's servants made a heavy canopy on the deck collapse on Agrippina's head. It killed Agrippina's servant, but Agrippina herself escaped death.

Then Nero's people gathered the crew on one side of the boat. The boat tilted and started sinking. Agrippina jumped into the water and swam to the shore. Nero's servants chased her, and hit her with a boat oar hoping to kill her, but she escaped. Once on the shore, she ran home, to her countryside villa. The news reached Nero, that she was alive. Terrified that she would start a revolt against him, he called his advisors, including Seneca, asking what to do. When Nero told them the truth, a long silence followed, says Tacitus. The advisors knew Agrippina was powerful and dangerous. "Seneca took the lead," says Tacitus, and asked "if the death order should be given to the military." Hearing this, Nero instantly went ahead and ordered Agrippina's death.

Covering Nero's crime, Seneca composed a letter to the Senate saying that Agrippina had planned to overthrow emperor Nero, and that the shipwreck was a sign that the gods themselves were trying to save the emperor.

Next Nero divorced his wife Octavia, and then had her killed to make his new love, Poppaea Sabina, happy. He married Poppaea. Soon, however, it was Poppaea's turn. In no time she was dead.

'Nero receives Octavia's head' by G.Muzzioli

In AD 64 a terrible fire broke out in Rome. It was rumored that the fire was started at the order of Nero who hated the ancient buildings and the narrow, crooked streets of the old city.

He needed more space to build a larger palace for himself. On the night the fire broke out, a few senators saw Nero's servants with torches in the streets, but didn't dare to stop them. The fire raged for six days and seven nights destroying hundreds of homes and temples. Suetonius says that Nero watched the disaster from a tall tower and praised "the beauty of the flames." He also dressed up in his theater costume and sang poetry about the flames of war.

To escape from accusations that he had caused the fire, Nero needed someone to blame. He chose the Christians. Jesus Christ had lived and died in the Roman province of Judaea. The period of Christ's ministry and death was during the reign of Tiberius, the second Emperor of Rome. At the time of the great fire in Rome, around 30 years after the death of Jesus, the number of Christians was rapidly growing in both Judaea and Rome. At that time Rome was *pagan*, non-Christian. It was only in AD 313 that the Roman emperor Constantine the Great would decree that Christians were free to practice their faith. Romans knew that Christians didn't believe in the Roman gods or god-emperors, and didn't have much respect for the Roman state. They were the perfect group to blame.

'Nero and the murder of Christians' by Karl von Piloty

Nero had hundreds of Christians rounded up and killed in extremely cruel ways. When he burned them alive or had them thrown to the wild beasts at the theater, Romans first cheered, but then fun gave way to feelings of pity. "It looked like Christians were being sacrificed not for the benefit of the country, but because of the cruelty of one man," reported Tacitus.

Once the fire was over, and many ancient buildings were gone, Nero built himself a gigantic palace. He called it the Golden House. Inside, by the entrance, there stood a colossal statue of the emperor, 120 feet (36 meters) high. Suetonius describes Nero's palace: "Inside the palace there were dining-rooms with ceilings of ivory. The ceiling panels could turn and shower down flowers and were fitted with pipes for sprinkling the guests with perfumes. The main banquet hall was circular and constantly revolved day and night, like the heavens. He had baths supplied with sea water." When the palace was finished, the ungrateful emperor didn't say a single word of approval or praise. His only words were, "Finally I have a decent house to live in."

By that time the Roman people hated Nero, and he was concerned about conspiracies against him. He asked the famous Oracle of Delphi when or how he would die. The oracle responded, "Look out for the seventy-third year." Nero was only 30, so he thought there was nothing to worry about.

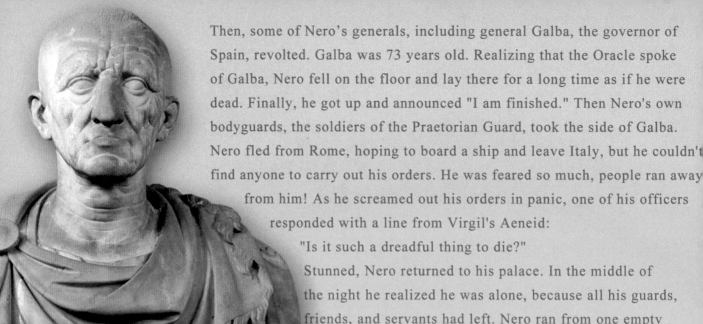

Then, some of Nero's generals, including general Galba, the governor of Spain, revolted. Galba was 73 years old. Realizing that the Oracle spoke of Galba, Nero fell on the floor and lay there for a long time as if he were dead. Finally, he got up and announced "I am finished." Then Nero's own bodyguards, the soldiers of the Praetorian Guard, took the side of Galba. Nero fled from Rome, hoping to board a ship and leave Italy, but he couldn't find anyone to carry out his orders. He was feared so much, people ran away from him! As he screamed out his orders in panic, one of his officers responded with a line from Virgil's Aeneid:

"Is it such a dreadful thing to die?"

Stunned, Nero returned to his palace. In the middle of the night he realized he was alone, because all his guards, friends, and servants had left. Nero ran from one empty palace room to another, calling for any man who knows how to use a sword. "Where are all the gladiators? Can't someone kill me?" he cried. "How can I have neither friends, nor enemies?" He left the palace again, deciding to jump into the Tiber River and drown — but became frightened and again ran back to the palace. He found a few loyal servants and secretly left the city together with them.

Servius Sulpicius Galba

In the countryside he ordered them to dig a grave for him. Soon they heard the news that the Senate had named Nero a public enemy and was planning to execute him by beating him to death. Nero ran around in panic, repeating "What an artist the world is losing!" He still believed he was the greatest poet and singer Rome had ever known. Finally, one of his servants killed him at Nero's own request.

'Nero's death' by Vasily Smirnov

When people heard that Nero was dead, there was so much happiness in Rome that celebrations continued all day and all night. Nero's name was erased from monuments. On paintings, his face was painted over. Galba was proclaimed the new emperor of Rome, but his rule was short as soon Galba, too, was killed. One after another, four men became rulers of Rome. The last of them, Vespasian, was a winner. He ruled Rome for 10 years.

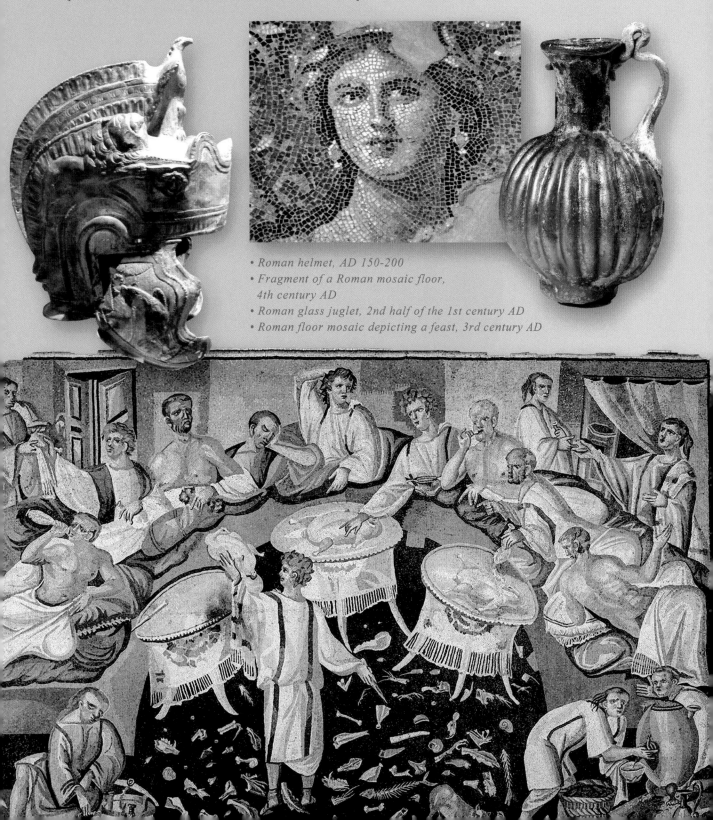

- *Roman helmet, AD 150-200*
- *Fragment of a Roman mosaic floor, 4th century AD*
- *Roman glass juglet, 2nd half of the 1st century AD*
- *Roman floor mosaic depicting a feast, 3rd century AD*

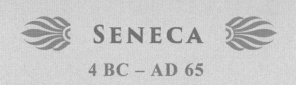

SENECA

4 BC – AD 65

Lucius Annaeus Seneca is a famous Roman philosopher who belonged to the philosophical school of *Stoicism*. The English word *stoical* means 'enduring hardships without complaining.' It comes from *stoicism*, a philosophy that originated in ancient Greece, and became popular in ancient Rome. The central idea of stoicism is that you can only achieve happiness if you follow the path of justice and fairness, and if your mind is free from both the desire of enjoyment and the fear of pain and hardships. The path to wisdom is self-control, said the Stoics. "True happiness is to enjoy the present moment," wrote Seneca, "without worrying about the future, and without feeling excited by hopes or depressed by fears. Happiness is to be satisfied with what we have, not wanting anything we don't have." Stoic philosophers also believed in fate: Whatever happens to you is not in your control, they said, and you have to accept your fate, even if it's cruel. "Count each separate day as a separate life" wrote Seneca.

*Seneca and Nero
by Eduardo Barrón*

Despite his wisdom, Seneca got involved in Roman politics, helping emperor Nero to preserve his power. He even grew rich from Nero's crimes. When Nero's stepbrother Britannicus was poisoned, the boy's wealth was divided up between Nero's friends, and part of it went to Seneca!

Seneca also was known to waste money just like his student Nero! According to Cassius Dio, he ordered "five hundred tables of citrus wood with legs of ivory, and he served banquets on them." In his book **On the Happy Life**, composed in AD 59, Seneca asks himself a question:
Can you be wise and waste money at the same time?
"Why do you drink precious expensive wine?" he asks himself.
"Why does your wife wear earrings whose price is more than a whole rich man's house?"
Seneca answers that even if you are imperfect, you can still try to reach for wisdom.
If you really want to escape your problems, what you need is not to escape to a different place, but to turn yourself into a different person!

When Nero sang in the theater, Seneca, who was his teacher, stood nearby and prompted him.
He also waved his hands and toga at Nero's every phrase to signal the audience to applaud.

'Emperor's box at the Roman circus' by Lawrence Alma-Tadema

"While this sort of child's play was going on in Rome," says Tacitus, "a terrible disaster occurred in Britain. Two cities were sacked by barbarians. Eighty thousand Romans perished, and the island of Britain was lost." The revolt in the Roman province of Britain was partly caused by... Seneca! Hoping to make some money, Seneca loaned an enormous amount of money to Britain. He was hoping to receive large interest payments on the loan, but then, for some reason, instead demanded all his money back! Seneca started punishing people who couldn't pay back their loans. A bloody revolt broke out in Britain over this. A politician named Publius Suillius accused Seneca of hypocrisy. "He is preaching justice and self-control, while sucking Roman provinces dry." Very soon Suillius was exiled from Rome.

Others, like historian Cassius Dio, defended Seneca. He had a positive influence on Nero, they said. He tried to prevent Nero from committing more crimes. Nero would have killed many more people, says Cassius Dio in his **Roman History**, had not Seneca said to him: "No matter how many you may kill, you cannot kill your successor." Seneca also said: "All cruelty comes from weakness." Was it wise for a philosopher to serve a crazy emperor? What do you think? Seneca once said, "Associate with people who are likely to improve you." And he was friends with Nero? Hmmm.... Remember the ancient Greek philosophers Plato and Aristotle who ran into problems trying to teach kings to be wise? Maybe Seneca, too, hoped to turn Nero into a wise king... As Nero's reign became more and more bizarre, Seneca tried to ignore the danger: "Man is affected not by events but by the view he takes of them," he wrote. But no matter what point of view he took, it was clear that Nero was leading his empire toward disaster.

'The arrival of the Caesar' by Ettore Forti

'Death of Seneca' by Manuel Domínguez Sánchez

Seneca moved to his countryside villa and worked on his books hoping that Nero would leave him alone. "Philosophy is a medicine for the wounds of life," he used to say. But Nero didn't want to let Seneca go, and twice refused to allow Seneca to retire from his service.

In AD 65, Seneca was caught up in a plot to kill Nero and make Roman politician Gaius Piso emperor. Some historians believed that Seneca was an active participant in the plot, and even intended to kill Piso, too, and make himself the emperor. Among Seneca's famous words are these: "Luck is what happens when preparation meets opportunity." Seneca was a fighter. "Throw me to the wolves and I will return leading the pack," he said. He was also a hard worker. In his words, "We hesitate to act, because we are afraid of difficulties... But actually, difficulties arise when we hesitate to act!"

The conspiracy failed, and Nero ordered Seneca to kill himself. Seneca did, using poison. His wife, Pompeia Paulina, didn't want to live without him and tried to die too, but Nero, who admired her loyalty and noble spirit, had his servants save her life against her will.

Roman grave altar

VESPASIAN

AD 9 – 79

Titus Flavius Vespasianus was the first Roman emperor who was not
related to the family of Julius Caesar. But ancient Roman historians
believed there were many signs that had predicted his great future.
The strangest of these signs was reported by Suetonius. During the
reign of Emperor Caligula, Vespasian held a government position
in Rome. Caligula noticed that the streets of Rome were
extremely dirty and blamed Vespasian. The emperor
was so angry, says Suetonius, that he ordered his
soldiers to pour mud on Vespasian as punishment
for the dirt in the streets. The soldiers heaped mud on
Vespasian dressed in his official white purple-bordered
toga. That wasn't a great day for Vespasian, but some
people interpreted that as a sign, says Suetonius. One day, they predicted, when Rome would be
treated like dirt by its enemies, Vespasian would carry it on his shoulders to clean and protect it!

While he clearly was not great as a local government official, Vespasian proved to be a great
military leader. As a legate of *Legio II Augusta* (Augustus' Second Legion) he became famous
during the Roman invasion of Britain. Another victory that brought him high military honors
was his suppression of the revolt in the Roman province of Judaea.

After the death of Nero and a year of civil wars, Vespasian was declared emperor.
Even as an emperor, he lived like a soldier. "His style of living was very far from costly,"
writes Cassius Dio. "He never spent more money than was absolutely necessary. The doors of his
palace stood open all day long and no guard was stationed at them."

Vespasian felt that men interested in luxury or fashion lacked manliness. "Once a young man reeking
of perfume came to thank him for being appointed to a government position," writes Suetonius.
"Vespasian turned away in disgust, and said 'I would rather you smelled of garlic!'"
"As the city was unsightly from fires and fallen buildings," continues Suetonius, "Vespasian allowed
anyone to take possession of empty lots and build on them. He began to rebuild the Capitol –
the square on the Capitoline Hill – by carrying away the rubble in his own hands." Vespasian was
a very confident man. Never upset about being criticized or laughed at, he valued sincerity more
than politeness.

"The only thing for which he can be seriously criticized," says Suetonius, "was his love of money... He increased the taxes paid by the Roman provinces, in some cases doubling them. He often used his position to buy grain and other supplies to immediately resell them at a profit." He took bribes right and left. "He sold government offices to candidates who were supposed to be elected," explains Suetonius, "and he sold acquitals to men who were in trouble with the law, whether innocent or guilty. He even appointed the most greedy and corrupt officials to the highest posts, so that they might be richer when he later condemned them and took away their wealth. In fact, it was common talk that he used these men as sponges, because he, so to speak, soaked them when they were dry and squeezed them when they were wet."

Despite being so greedy and corrupt, "Vespasian was most generous to all citizens," says Suetonius. He increased salaries and created pensions for senators and retired consuls, he donated money to rebuild cities that had suffered from earthquakes and fires, and "generously helped men of talent and artists." He even ordered that teachers of Latin and Greek rhetoric – public speaking – be paid by the government! A mechanical engineer invented a way to transport heavy columns to the Capitol more cheaply. He offered his brilliant invention to Vespasian. Vespasian paid the engineer generously, but refused to make use of it. "I need to feed the poor," he explained, "your invention would take their jobs away."

Most ancient cultures had a very different view of good and evil compared to what we consider good and evil today. The value of human life was low. The wealth of Rome was built on the labor, suffering, and sacrifice of hundreds of thousands of slaves, soldiers, and common people in the Roman Provinces who lived in poverty and paid taxes to Rome. But the Romans felt this was the way the world should be, the way it had always been. Most of them never thought of their society as cruel. They believed the Roman state was the only source of order on Earth, and that the rest of the world was a dangerous mess. Vespasian, who was generous and kind to Romans, suppressed rebellions in the Roman provinces with unbelievable cruelty. When he defeated rebels in Judaea he executed thousands and thousands of people as punishment. They were not soldiers killed in battle – it was just an act of cruelty performed to teach all Roman provinces to obey Rome. Today, we think of such slaughter as a war crime, as evil, but in the days of ancient Rome nobody called Vespasian a war criminal. They thought of him as a hero who made the Roman state stronger.

They say that Vespasian had a great sense of humor. He was famous for his jokes, and he often made fun of his own love of money. Once on a journey, a driver of Vespasian's carriage suddenly announced the mules who pulled the carriage needed new horse shoes. As the carriage stopped, a man approached the emperor asking for help with a lawsuit. Vespasian guessed that the man had bribed the driver to stop the emperor's carriage. Instead of punishing the driver, he asked how much had been paid, and made the driver pay him half!

Cassius Dio reports that when the Senate voted to erect a statue of Vespasian that cost a fortune, Vespasian held out his hand and said: "See this hand? Use it as the base for the statue, and put the money right here."

To the horror of his friends and family, Vespasian decided to tax public toilets! His son Titus couldn't believe his dad was that cheap. When Vespasian heard what Titus had to say about this, he grabbed some money he had received as toilet tax and made Titus smell it.
"Does it smell of toilet?" he asked. "No," said Titus. "Exactly," said Vespasian.
"Money doesn't smell." These words became a famous saying. Its meaning is:
Money doesn't lose its value even if it comes from a shameful or criminal deal.

Vespasian's sons Domitian and Titus took bribes and sold government positions just like their dad. They acted like they were kings of Roman provinces, says Cassius Dio. So great was their power, that Vespasian made fun of it by sending the following message to Domitian: "I thank you, my son, for permitting me to hold the emperor's office and for not overthrowing me... at least for now!"

Portrait of Vespasian carved in amethyst   *Ancient public toilet excavated in Rome*

*One of the best-preserved ancient Roman temples in Nîmes, the south of France,
built in AD 4 in honor of Caesar Augustus' grandsons, and a Roman glass jug, 1st century AD*

Finally, Vespasian fell sick. His doctors thought he was going to die. There was a bad sign, they told him: "We've seen a comet with a long tail," and that often meant someone important was going to die. "Long tail?" asked Vespasian, "This sign is not for me, it's for some king with long hair. I am bald!" He couldn't stop joking even on his deathbed. They say that when he finally knew he was going to die, he said, "I feel like I am already becoming a god," making fun of the Romans' custom of declaring dead emperors gods.

Jokes continued even at Vespasian's funeral. At Roman funerals they often hired actors to wear the mask of the person who was being buried, and to say words, or read speeches, for which that person was known. At Vespasian's funeral a famous actor who wore his mask asked in a loud voice "How much does my funeral cost?" "Ten million sesterces," was the answer. "Oh no," cried out the actor, "Give that money to me, and you can just toss me into the Tiber River without any funeral!"

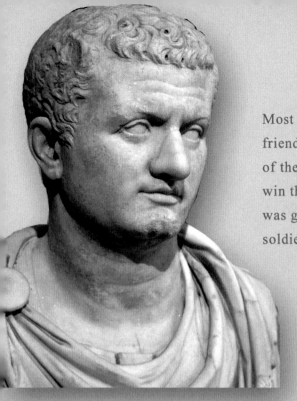

Most Roman historians praised the Emperor Titus for being nice, friendly, and loyal to his friends. "Titus was the delight and darling of the human race," says Suetonius, "such surpassing ability had he to win the friendship of all men... His memory was extraordinary and he was great in all the arts, both of war and of peace. He was a skilled soldier, and he also wrote great speeches and poems in Latin and Greek. He was a good singer, and played the harp quite well. "Titus could also imitate anyone's handwriting. He could fake any signature and often joked that he would make a good criminal. Titus was raised in Rome. His best friend in childhood was Britannicus, Nero's stepbrother. When Britannicus was poisoned by Nero, Titus was sitting next to him at dinner. He also took a sip from the poisoned cup, says Suetonius, and was sick for a long time, but survived. Titus never forgot Britannicus, and years later set up a golden statue of Britannicus in his palace.

Titus was a good emperor, according to Suetonius, even though his reign was only two years. "When people came to him asking for help, he had a rule: "never let anyone go away without hope." One day at dinner he remembered that he had done nothing for anybody that day. "Friends, I have lost a day," he said. Like his dad, Titus was confident in his power. When two men of patrician families were found guilty of plotting against him, he decided not to punish them. "He told them the emperor's power was the gift of fate," wrote Suetonius, "and promised to give them anything they wanted as long as they gave up their conspiracy." He even sent a messenger to the mother of one of the conspirators who lived outside Rome to tell her not to worry about her son.

Titus is remembered mostly for two events – both historic disasters. The first is the destruction of Jerusalem and the Jerusalem temple. It happened when Vespasian was still the emperor.

Jerusalem and its temple had been the center of the Jewish faith, culture, and civilization of ancient Israel since around 1000 BC. Led by Pompey the Great, the Romans conquered Israel and captured Jerusalem in 63 BC. In AD 6 they made it the Roman province of Judaea.

Rome forced their provinces to pay heavy taxes, and starting in AD 66 a number of anti-Roman riots broke out in Judea, ending in an all-out war. Vespasian suppressed rebellions in smaller towns, but didn't want to attack Jerusalem. Jerusalem was a powerful fortress with three walls, underground tunnels, and fortifications. Vespasian was afraid that the siege of Jerusalem would cost too many Roman lives. But when Vespasian became the emperor and was busy in Rome, he left it to Titus to take care of the province of Judaea. Titus conquered one town after another, and soon arrived at the walls of Jerusalem.

Jerusalem was so well protected that the Roman army had no hope of taking it by direct attack. So a long siege of Jerusalem began instead. The Romans dug a trench all around the walls of Jerusalem and built a wall just as high as the Jerusalem walls. They killed anyone who tried to flee the city by crucifying them on top of the Roman wall where all the defenders of Jerusalem could see. Up to 500 crucifixions were happening every day. The defenders of Jerusalem did not give up. They managed to hold out for an entire year. "They had underground tunnels dug from inside the city extending out under the walls to distant points in the country," says Cassius Dio, "and going out through them, they attacked the Romans..."
Finally, the Roman soldiers used their war machines to break through the walls of Jerusalem.

'Destruction of the Temple of Jerusalem' by, Francesco Hayez

Tacitus says that Titus gathered a council to decide whether to destroy the great Jerusalem Temple that stood on the Temple Mount in the heart of the city. His advisors thought the Temple was a holy site and that the Romans should save it. But Titus pointed out that the only religions that considered the Jerusalem Temple sacred were Judaism and Christianity. Titus hated both, and ordered the complete destruction of the Temple.

"While the holy house was on fire," wrote Jewish historian Josephus who was one of the early leaders of the Jewish revolt against the Romans "everything was plundered ... and the ground was not even visible under the dead bodies that lay on it... The Romans also burned down the treasury chambers after first taking all the money and precious goods of the Temple. The Roman soldiers had so much gold in their hands, that in nearby Syria a pound of gold sold for only half its usual price."

'The Triumph of Titus'
by Lawrence Alma-Tadema

A relief from the Arch of Titus in Rome showing the treasures taken from the Jerusalem Temple

Triumphal Arch of Titus and a silver cup depicting a Triumph

After Titus became the emperor, another historic disaster occurred – the eruption of Mount Vesuvius, an active volcano that completely destroyed the cities of Herculaneum and Pompeii. "There were frequent rumblings," wrote Cassius Dio, "some were under the ground and sounded like thunder... Then suddenly a loud crash was heard, and huge stones shot out of Mount Vesuvius... Then came great fire and endless smoke that eclipsed the sun. A huge quantity of ash was blown out, which covered both sea and land and filled all the air. Two entire cities, Herculaneum and Pompeii, were buried under the ashes. This happened while many people of Pompeii were sitting at the theater enjoying a show."

Modern scientists say that the eruption of Vesuvius started with a rain of stones spewed out by the volcano. The stone rain continued for 18 hours, and during that time most people who lived in Herculaneum and Pompeii managed to escape. The next day blazing hot clouds of ash burst out of the crater of the volcano. The ash destroyed and buried all the buildings in the two cities, killing everyone who had stayed behind.

'The last day of Pompeii' by Karl Brullov

Titus loved gladiator fights and staged some of the most expensive circus shows in Roman history. He finished the construction of the **Colosseum**, a huge theater in the center of Rome. The construction was begun under the emperor Vespasian in AD 72, and took 8 years. The Colosseum could seat 50,000 spectators. Below the Colosseum were underground passages to bring animals, actors, and gladiators to the middle of the arena. The Colosseum had 76 entrances and exits. Spectators bought tickets that said which entrance they were supposed to use. Slaves, former gladiators, actors, and gravediggers were prohibited from coming to the Colosseum The west exit was called the Gate of Death: That's where dead gladiators were carried out of the arena. Huge building projects, like the Colosseum, were one of the ways Roman politicians and emperors won the support of the people of Rome. They created a lot of temporary jobs to keep people busy and paid. And, of course, there were distractions like 'bread and circuses.'

'The Colosseum' by Lawrence Alma-Tadema

Titus' sestertius coin depicting the Colosseum

To please the crowds, every Roman emperor added new public holidays, until the Romans spent half their days watching gladiators, public executions, and chariot races at the circus.

Titus died of sickness. There were rumors that he was poisoned by his younger brother Domitian, who became the next emperor.

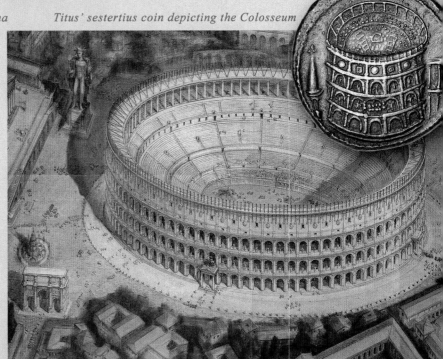

TRAJAN

AD 53 – 117

Trajan is considered one of the *five good emperors* of Rome, during whose reigns the empire enjoyed peace and growth. Trajan was a Roman general, very popular with the army. He was adopted by emperor Nerva who had no kids, and became the emperor in AD 98. Trajan is best known for his building program throughout the Roman Empire. New bridges, aqueducts, roads, squares, public buildings, and canals were built during his reign all over Italy and in the Roman provinces. Trajan's Bridge over the Danube River was the longest arch bridge in the world for over 1000 years. Trajan built a new Forum in Rome. Trajan's column, a monument built in honor of one of Trajan's military victories, still stands in modern-day Rome.

Trajan believed that honor was more important than power. "Trajan became famous for his justice, for his bravery, and for the simplicity of his habits," writes Cassius Dio. When Trajan's wife, Pompeia Plotina, first entered the emperor's palace in Rome, she looked back at the crowd of people who were watching her and said, "One day I will leave this palace, and I will be the same woman who is walking into it now." Like Trajan, she believed that power should not change a person. When Trajan became emperor he handed a sword to the head of the Praetorian Guard - the emperor's bodyguards - and said: "Take this sword, and if I rule well, use it to defend me, but if my rule is evil, use it against me."

Digital reconstruction of the Forum of Trajan in Rome by Macrons

Like Roman rulers before him, Trajan encouraged the persecution of Christians. Pliny the Younger, a Roman author and the governor of the Roman province of Bithynia-Pontus (in modern Turkey) sent letters to the emperor, reporting about his work and asking for advice.

In one of his letters he writes:

"I have never been present at any trial of the Christians, and I do not know, therefore, what is the usual punishment for being a Christian... I am wondering if I should punish the old and the weak as severely as the young and the strong... and if they give up their faith, should they be pardoned?... This is how I deal with the Christians who have been brought before me. I ask them whether they are Christians; if they say yes, then I repeat the question a second and a third time, warning them of the punishment for being a Christian, and if they still persist, I order them to be taken away to prison. ...Those who deny that they are Christians and call upon the Roman gods repeating the words after me, and those who worship your image and the statues of our gods - all those I let go, especially if they agree to curse the name of Christ, which, it is said, those who are really Christians would never do... Many persons of all ages, and of both sexes alike, are being brought to me, accused of being Christians. The disease of Christianity has spread not only through the cities, but into the villages and the rural districts..."

Answering Pliny's letter, Emperor Trajan wrote: "You have adopted the proper course, my dear Pliny If Christians are brought before you, they are to be punished. But if any one denies that he is

a Christian and makes it clear that he is not by offering prayers to our gods, then he is to be pardoned."

After Trajan, every new Roman emperor was greeted with the words, "May you be luckier than Augustus and better than Trajan," since Augustus and Trajan were considered the best emperors the empire had.

The Senate declared Trajan *Optimus Princeps* – the best ruler. By the time of Trajan's death the territory of the Roman Empire was the biggest in its history. Latin, the language of ancient Rome, spread throughout Western Europe. It mixed with the languages of the Roman provinces and gave rise to the *Romance languages* – such as French, Spanish, Portuguese, Italian, and Romanian.

Reliefs covering the Column of Trajan and a Roman oil lamp, 1st century AD

MARCUS AURELIUS

AD 121-180

Marcus Aurelius was a Stoic philosopher and a Roman Emperor
who ruled between 161 and 180. He was the last emperor of
the **Pax Romana** (the Roman Peace), a 200-year-long period
of Roman history when the Roman empire grew and successfully
ruled most of Europe. Marcus Aurelius was a grand nephew
of emperor Hadrian, and nephew of emperor Antoninus Pius
who ruled after Hadrian and made Marcus his heir.
Marcus Aurelius studied philosophy even as a child.
When he was 14 he started wearing a simple
Greek-style cloak and sleeping on the ground like
many stoic philosophers who despised comfort and
luxury. "From my grandfather I have learned to be
gentle and stay away from anger and greed,"
wrote Marcus Aurelius. "I have learned from him

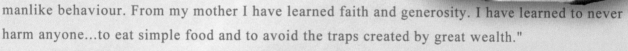

manlike behaviour. From my mother I have learned faith and generosity. I have learned to never
harm anyone...to eat simple food and to avoid the traps created by great wealth."
"If you think of every action in life as though it were your last, you will stop doing useless things,"
Marcus Aurelius advised in his book **Meditations.**
When Marcus Aurelius was 17 he became the heir to the throne, and had to move to the imperial
palace. He believed that the life of power and luxury corrupts one's character, but had no choice.
'Where life is possible, then it is possible to live the right life," he wrote in **Meditations**.
"Life is possible in a palace, so it is possible to live the right life in a palace."

When the time came for Marcus to become emperor, he demanded that his brother Lucius become
emperor too. "Marcus was not physically strong, and he spent most of his time studying and writing,"
says Cassius Dio, "while his brother Lucius was younger, full of energy, loved sports, and had
the skills to be a military leader." So for the first time in its history Rome had two emperors who
ruled together. The people of Rome loved the new emperors because they dressed, talked, and
behaved like everyone else, not trying to look like god-like characters far above the common people.
Marcus Aurelius thought of being an emperor as a job. He didn't like it, but he did it well.
"In the morning, when you have trouble getting out of bed," he wrote," tell yourself: I have to go
to work – as a human being. Nothing to complain about. I am going to do the things I came into
the world to do. I didn't come into the world in order to huddle under the blankets and stay warm."

As always, Roman provinces kept rioting against Roman rule, and Marcus Aurelius kept sending Roman troops to suppress the riots. He fought a few wars – in Syria, in Armenia, and in Parthia (ancient Iran). The most persistent enemies were the German tribes in the north. They raided the border of the empire in Gaul. After a long struggle and many losses, the Romans managed to push them back. The Germans were skilled warriors and trained both men and women for war. After one battle, "among the dead bodies of the barbarians Romans found even women's bodies in armor," says Cassius Dio.

Marcus and Lucius ruled together until AD 162 when Lucius was sent to fight the war in Syria. Roman historians hinted that the real reason for Lucius' departure was different. Unlike his brother, Lucius loved parties, wasted a lot of money on festivals and gladiator fights, and didn't pay as much attention to his work as he should have. Marcus and the Senate thought that leading the army was a better job for him.

Lucius Verus

'Goth soldiers cross a river' by Evariste-Vital Luminais

Cassius Dio tells a story of a conspiracy against Marcus Aurelius. The emperor fell ill, and his wife Faustina thought he might die. Their son, Commodus, was too young to become an emperor. Scared for their future, Faustina made a deal with the Roman governor of Syria, Cassius, asking him to declare himself an emperor at the news of Marcus' death. Once declared an emperor, he would marry her and adopt Commodus as the heir to the throne. Cassius was a friend of Marcus Aurelius and Faustina, and he agreed. They kept their deal secret. Soon Cassius heard a rumor of Marcus Aurelius' death, and declared himself emperor. But the rumor was false. After he learned the truth, Cassius was disappointed and didn't want to give up his hope for the throne. He gathered his troops and prepared for a civil war against Marcus Aurelius.

Marcus Aurelius felt betrayed. Addressing his soldiers and the Senate, he said," I would gladly have given the power of the emperor to Cassius without a struggle for the good of the State... because I am old and weak." But Cassius had proven untrustworthy. Still Marcus Aurelius didn't want to fight him. There is a prize better than victory, he said. "It's to forgive a man who has done evil, to remain a friend to one who has betrayed friendship, and to remain loyal to him who has disrespected loyalty." But Marcus Aurelius didn't get a chance to forgive Cassius. Cassius perished, killed by soldiers loyal to the emperor. Faustina also died, and Marcus Aurelius burned all the letters of Cassius and Faustina without reading them. He didn't want to learn the names of any other people who were involved in the conspiracy, so he didn't have to punish anyone.

Marcus Aurelius believed that we should train our minds to focus on positive things. "The things you think about determine the quality of your mind," he wrote.

"Your soul takes on the color of your thoughts."

The emperor was very sad at the loss of Faustina. Cassius Dio writes: "He ordered that a golden statue of Faustina should be carried in a chair into the theatre on every occasion when the emperor came to see a show. The statue was to be put in the same place where Faustina used to sit, with women from the top Roman families sitting around her."
When Marcus died, his son Commodus became the next Roman Emperor.

Faustina

Roman marble floor, 1st century BC

There were about 25 emperors in a 50-year period of Roman history known as the *Crisis of the Third Century*. During the reign of Emperor Diocletian (AD 284-305) the empire was split in two - the Eastern and the Western portions. The emperor who unified Rome again, was Flavius Valerius Constantinus, or Constantine the Great. He was also to become the first Christian emperor of Rome.

As a kid Constantine lived at the court of Emperor Diocletian. His dad was a popular Roman general, always fighting wars in faraway Roman provinces. The reason Diocletian wanted Constantine to live at his court was to ensure that Constantine's dad stayed loyal to the emperor. So, even though he lived in luxury, Constantine was a hostage. Diocletian became known for the persecution and murder of Christians. Constantine never forgot seeing the deaths of thousands of innocent people. His mother, Helena, became a Christian.

When Constantine grew up, he served in the Roman army and became a successful military leader. After the death of Diocletian, Diocletian's son Galerius became the emperor. Galerius saw Constantine as a rival and tried to have him killed a few times, but Constantine always survived. Finally Constantine fled and joined his father in Gaul, in the Western Roman Empire. He fought alongside his father defending the empire from the growing power of the barbarians – the Franks, the Goths, the Vandals, and other northern tribes.

When his father became ill, he named Constantine the Emperor of his portion of the Western Roman Empire, which included Britain, Gaul, and Spain. Constantine was a good ruler. He built cities, roads, public buildings, and fortresses. He also put an end to the persecution of Christians in his territory. Diocletian's son Galerius continued murdering Christians until his death in 311. He died of cancer. On his deathbed, Galerius repented for his cruelty toward Christians and canceled all his anti-Christian orders before he died. A civil war broke out. Constantine and his legions approached Rome in 312, but Constantine's army was only about half the size of the army of his rivals.

On the day before the battle for Rome, Constantine looked at the sky and thought he saw the sign of the cross over the sun. "An amazing sign appeared to him from heaven," wrote Eusebius, the author of *The Life of Constantine.* "About noon he saw with his own eyes a cross of light in the heavens, above the sun, and he also saw the words, *In Hoc Signo Vinces* – 'with this sign you will win.' At this sight he was struck with amazement, and so was his whole army that witnessed that miracle.

'Constantine's vision of the cross' fresco by Raphael

That night Constantine had a dream. In his dream Jesus Christ appeared before him telling him to carry the sign of the cross into battle. Roman legions usually carried an *aquila*, or 'an eagle standard,' a decorated pole with an image of an eagle on top. Each legion had an aquila, carried by a special 'eagle-bearer.' Constantine ordered that the eagle standards of his legions be replaced by standards topped with crosses. His soldiers also painted crosses on their shields. Constantine was wearing a helmet with the *christogram* - the first two letters of the Greek word *Christ* – ΧΡΙΣΤΟΣ (Christos) - X and P. Constantine won the Battle of the Milvian Bridge and took control of Rome. But the empire was not yet unified.

a Christogram

'Battle of the Milvian Bridge' by Giulio Romano

The eastern portion of it was ruled by the Roman general Licinius. Licinius followed the example of Constantine and put crosses on the standards and shields of his troops. Despite the persecutions, the number of Christians was growing, and Licinius needed their support. In 313, Constantine and Licinius signed the *Edict of Milan* which stated that Christians would no longer be persecuted in the Roman Empire. But only 7 years later, Licinius started persecuting Christians again.

First he forbade church councils, then declared that men and women couldn't go to church services together. Then he announced that if any army officer refused to offer sacrifices to the Roman gods, he would lose his job, and if a prisoner in jail refused to worship Roman gods he would not be fed. Finally Licinius started openly murdering Christian bishops and burning churches. "Some suffered a new kind of death," wrote Eusebius, "having their bodies cut into pieces, and, after this cruel punishment, more horrible than anything done before, being cast, as a food to fishes, into the depths of the sea."

Constantine declared war against Licinius, and after several battles Licinius was defeated. In 324 Constantine became the ruler of the unified Roman Empire. He was 52.
In 330 Constantine founded a new capital of the Roman Empire on the location of the ancient city of Byzantium. He named the new city Constantinople. It became the capital of the Empire for more than a thousand years.

After he became emperor, Constantine sent his mother, Helena, to the Holy Land - the land of ancient Israel, to learn about the life and teachings of Jesus. Helena found pieces of the cross that Jesus was crucified on, and built a church in Bethlehem where Jesus had been born.
Even though Constantine was not baptized as a Christian until shortly before his death, he behaved like a Christian ruler. He built churches. He prohibited going to fortune-tellers. He stopped gladiator fights. He prohibited executing criminals through crucifixion. He closed many temples of Roman gods, seizing their treasures. Temple sacrifices were forbidden. Constantinople "was filled with statues of the most spectacular workmanship," writes Eusebius, "which people, deceived by pagan religion, had long honored as gods...The temple priests were ordered, amid general laughter and scorn, to bring their gods from the darkness of the temples into the light of day, into the street. The statues were stripped of their ornaments, so everyone could see the ugly reality under the painted surface - that these were just statues, not gods."

Constantine called on wealthy Romans to abandon their wasteful lifestyles. Eusebius says that one day, talking to a man known for his greed, Constantine asked him,"How far, my friend, can we carry our wealth with us?" Then, with a tip of a spear he drew a rectangle on the ground. It was the size and shape of a grave. "Even if you capture the whole wealth of this world," he said, "you will end up having no more than this little spot which I have marked out, if indeed even that will be yours."

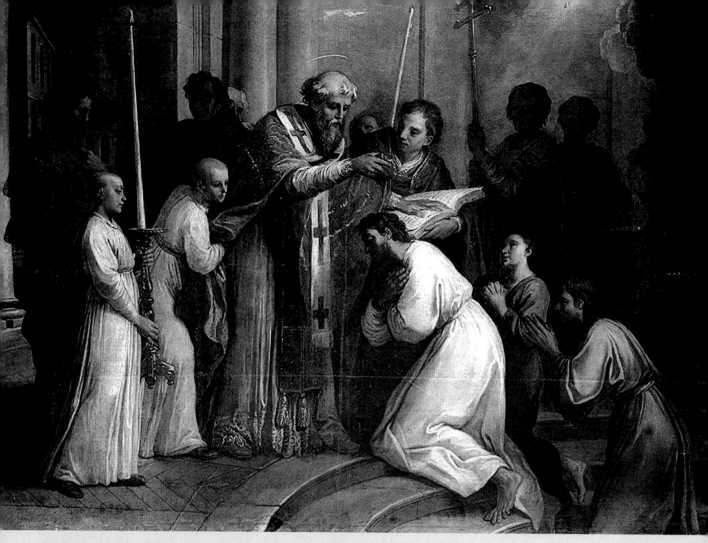

'The Baptism of Constantine' by Louis de Boullogne the Younger

Constantine invited leaders of Christian communities to unite by holding a church council in the town of Nicaea. There, they created the famous statement of Christian belief called the Nicene Creed. The opening words of the Nicene Creed state: "I believe in one God, the Father Almighty, Creator of heaven and earth, of all things visible and invisible; and in one Lord Jesus Christ, Son of God, born of the Father before all ages..."

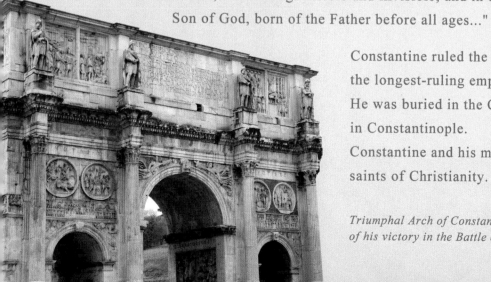

Constantine ruled the Roman Empire for 31 years, the longest-ruling emperor except for Augustus. He was buried in the Church of the Holy Apostles in Constantinople.

Constantine and his mother Helena were declared saints of Christianity.

Triumphal Arch of Constantine in Rome built in honor of his victory in the Battle of the Milvian Bridge

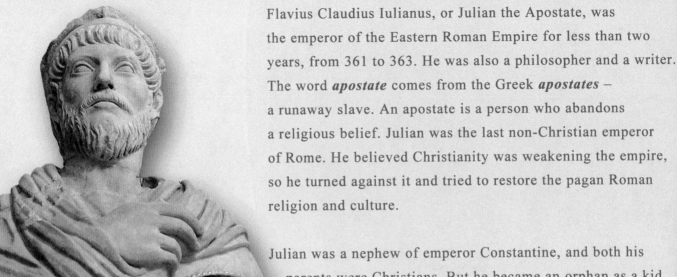

Flavius Claudius Iulianus, or Julian the Apostate, was the emperor of the Eastern Roman Empire for less than two years, from 361 to 363. He was also a philosopher and a writer. The word *apostate* comes from the Greek *apostates* – a runaway slave. An apostate is a person who abandons a religious belief. Julian was the last non-Christian emperor of Rome. He believed Christianity was weakening the empire, so he turned against it and tried to restore the pagan Roman religion and culture.

Julian was a nephew of emperor Constantine, and both his parents were Christians. But he became an orphan as a kid and was raised by his parents' slave, Mardonius, who was a foreigner, from a Gothic tribe in the North. As descendants of Constantine fought for power and influence, Julian, who was 18, was sent into exile to the Greek province of Cappadocia. There he met the Christian bishop George of Cappadocia, who had an excellent private library and lent Julian books by ancient Greek and Roman authors. The bishop had no idea that the study of the classical Greek and Roman literature and philosophy would influence Julian to abandon his Christian faith. Two years later Julian started worshipping the Greek sun god Helios and other Greek and Roman gods.

Julian was appointed emperor of the Western portion of the Roman empire by emperor Constantius II, the son of Constantine the Great. Julian's main job was to push away invasions of Germanic tribes in Gaul. He was successful and popular with his troops. While at war, he didn't give up studying philosophy and literature. He got up in the middle of the night to read. His bed was a simple rough rug and a blanket, says historian Ammianus Marcellinus. The first thing he did when he woke up was to secretly pray to Mercury, the Roman messenger god, "the swift intelligence of the universe."

"To win the favor of all men and have opposition from none, Julian pretended to be a follower of Christianity, against which he had long since secretly revolted," explains Marcellinus, "He asked the advice of fortune-tellers and practiced many customs of pagan worshippers. But in order to conceal this, on the feast of the Epiphany which the Christians celebrate in the month of January, Julian went to their church, and prayed to their God in the usual manner."

The relationship between Julian and Constantius grew tense, and they were about to start a civil war when Constantius died, and Julian became the ruler of the entire Roman Empire.

Back in Constantinople, Julian was shocked by the luxury and greed that had taken hold of the emperor's court. Some top officials were "fattened on the robbery of temples and scenting out gain from every source," says Marcellinus. "Many of them rose from complete poverty to enormous wealth, and knew no limit to bribery, robbery, and extravagance, always ready to seize the property of others." There were feasts and banquets every day, and instead of being proud of triumphs won in battle, they bragged about what they ate at dinner! Julian called for a barber to trim his hair. The barber showed up dressed in such expensive and luxurious clothes, that Julian exclaimed, "I sent for a barber, not for a banker!" He fired dozens of palace servants, guards, and cooks overpaid for their jobs.

Julian also decided it was time to restore the ancient religion of Rome. He ordered the temples to be reopened, all the temples destroyed during Constantine's reign rebuilt, and the worship of the Roman gods restored.

Julian noticed that Christianity was spreading especially fast in hard times - during epidemic diseases, fires, and earthquakes. That was because Christians practiced compassion. In hard times they helped not only their own families, but all people - Christian or pagan. Writing to a friend who was a pagan priest, Julian complained, "They support not only their poor but ours as well, and all men see that we don't help our own people, but they help everyone." Julian hoped that pagan priests could imitate the Christians so that the old Roman religion could come to life again. "Why don't we realize that it's the kindness of Christians to strangers, and their wise lifestyle that has made their religion popular?" wrote Julian."We should practice these things. Make your priests good by shaming them, persuade them to behave this way, or fire them!" To compete with Christianity, Julian was planning to open inns for poor travelers, and give money and grain to the poor. But it looked like that battle couldn't be won. People changed their life right away when they became Christians, but if they kept their pagan beliefs, they were uninterested in charity and works of kindness.

In 362 Julian issued a law proclaiming freedom of religion. It said every religion was equal in the eyes of the law. However, when two of his bodyguards, Juventinus and Maximinus, both Christians, were overheard at a party, criticizing Julian's religious laws, they were executed in the middle of the night.

Soon Julian went to war again, this time against the Persian Sassanid Empire invading the Roman Empire from the East. In one of the battles against the Persians Julian was wounded and died. Legend says that his last words were addressed to Jesus Christ: "You have won, Galilean," he said.

Theodosius the First was the last emperor to rule over both the Eastern and Western portions of the Roman Empire. He became emperor in 379, and in 380 he had himself baptized as Christian when a serious illness threatened his life. That same year Theodosius made Christianity the official religion of the Roman Empire. Eager to erase the Roman religion that inspired their persecution, Christians started consistently destroying Roman and Greek temples. The famous Temple of Apollo in Delphi, the seat of the Delphi Oracle, was demolished. In 393 Theodosius issued a law that prohibited any public non-Christian religious customs. One of his laws even prohibited any public discussion of any religious questions! He also put an end to pagan rituals at the Olympic Games, and some historians believe that it was during his reign that the Olympic Games were discontinued altogether.

During his reign the power of the barbarians, who kept invading the empire from the north, grew to such an extent, that Theodosius gave up the idea of defeating them. He started making agreements with Goths and Franks, and opened the borders of the empire, allowing whole armies of foreigners to settle in Italy and Greece. Theodosius hoped that the barbarians would help defend the borders of the empire. Instead, allowing them in resulted in clashes between barbarian migrants and locals, in revolts, and many deaths. In 376, the Goths asked Rome to allow them to cross the Danube river and settle in the Roman Empire to escape from the Huns led by Atilla the Hun. 200,000 Goth refugees were allowed to live in Italy and Greece.

In 390 the people of the Greek city of Thessalonica rioted against the Gothic troops who had settled in the city. The Greek chariot racing champion was thrown in jail by the Goths. In response, the rioters killed the Goth commander. Theodosius refused to admit that letting barbarians settle in Roman cities was a bad policy. Angry, he ordered revenge on the people of Thessalonica. When the citizens of Thessalonica were gathered in their arena to watch a chariot race, the gates were locked, and Gothic soldiers sent in. They killed everyone in the arena. Roman historian Theodoret wrote that "seven thousand perished without any court sentence passed upon them. Like stalks of wheat at the time of harvest, they were all cut down."

Ambrose, the bishop of Milan, excommunicated Theodosius for this evil act. *Excommunication* is a punishment prohibiting a member of the Christian church from receiving the *sacrament of communion*. Here is how Theodoret describes this event: "When Ambrose heard of this catastrophe, he went out to meet the Emperor, who desired, as usual, to enter the holy church. But Ambrose didn't let him in, saying 'Emperor, you behave as if you are unaware of your guilt in having caused this great massacre. But now that you are not that angry anymore, don't you see how enormous your crime is? ... People you rule, Emperor, are of the same nature as yourself, and they are your fellow servants, for there is only one Lord and Ruler of all - the One who created both people and kings. So how dare you lift up in prayer hands soaked in the blood of the innocent?'"

"The Emperor shut himself up in his palace and shed floods of tears," says Theodoret. Ambrose ordered Theodosius to wear a burial shroud instead of his royal clothes, and publicly beg God for forgiveness. Theodosius obeyed. Ambrose also advised that any death sentence signed by Theodosius should be delayed by 30 days, and confirmed again at the end of that term – to make sure the decision was not guided by anger. The emperor obeyed. It was the first time in Roman history that the church proved more powerful than the emperor. Less than a century earlier Christians were being persecuted and their churches burned by Roman emperors!

When Ambrose finally allowed Theodosius to enter church again, Theodosius was so ashamed and sorry for his crimes, that he "prayed neither standing, nor kneeling, but threw himself face down on the floor. He tore his hair, struck his forehead, and cried, asking God for forgiveness." After Theodosius' death his Gothic troops and settlers betrayed the Romans and raided Roman towns as far East as Constantinople, killing Romans and plundering Roman homes. Theodosius' two sons, only 18 and 10 years old, were unable to keep the empire together.

'Theodosius and Ambrose' by Anthonis Van Dyck

From that time on, the empire was permanently divided into the Western Roman Empire with its capital in Rome, and the Eastern Roman Empire, with its center in Constantinople.

Many historians mark the day of Theodosius' death as the end of ancient Rome. The Western Roman Empire began to fall apart in the early 5th century, overwhelmed by Germanic migrants and endless invasions. So many migrants from Germanic tribes hostile to the Romans had settled in Italy, that the Roman government couldn't keep them under the rule of the Roman law. They rioted, attacked the Romans, joined forces with newly-invading enemies, and finally brought the end of the Roman Empire. In 410 Visigoths invaded and sacked Rome, enslaving its population and burning the city.

In 476 AD, Germanic barbarian tribal leader Odoacer conquered Rome. He forced the last emperor of Rome, Romulus Augustulus, to give up his crown. Without a strong government, education, or culture, Western Europe entered the 500-year-long period known as The Dark Ages.

The Eastern Roman Empire, also called the Byzantine Empire, continued to exist for another thousand years. But finally, it too fell to invaders. In 1453 its last emperor, Constantine XI Palaiologos perished during the Siege of Constantinople by the Ottoman Turks – Muslim invaders from the east who had been attacking the Eastern Roman Empire for 500 years. Constantinople became the capital of the Ottoman Empire. In 1923, as the new nation of Turkey was being created out of the remains of the dying Ottoman Empire, the city name Constantinople was changed to Istanbul.

'The Course Of Empire - Destruction' by Thomas Cole

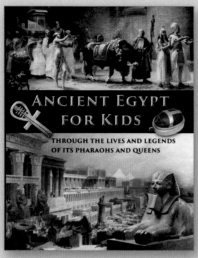

ANCIENT EGYPT FOR KIDS

THROUGH THE LIVES AND LEGENDS OF ITS PHARAOHS AND QUEENS

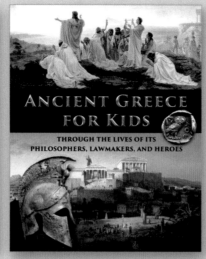

ANCIENT GREECE FOR KIDS

THROUGH THE LIVES OF ITS PHILOSOPHERS, LAWMAKERS, AND HEROES

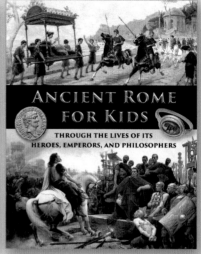

ANCIENT ROME FOR KIDS

THROUGH THE LIVES OF ITS HEROES, EMPERORS, AND PHILOSOPHERS

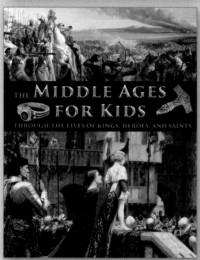

THE MIDDLE AGES FOR KIDS

THROUGH THE LIVES OF KINGS, HEROES, AND SAINTS

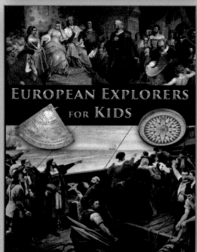

EUROPEAN EXPLORERS FOR KIDS

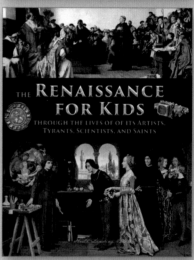

THE RENAISSANCE FOR KIDS

THROUGH THE LIVES OF OF ITS ARTISTS, TYRANTS, SCIENTISTS, AND SAINTS

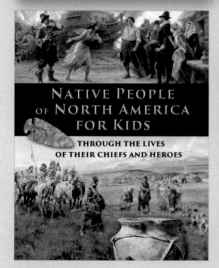

NATIVE PEOPLE OF NORTH AMERICA FOR KIDS

THROUGH THE LIVES OF THEIR CHIEFS AND HEROES

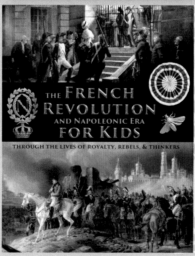

THE FRENCH REVOLUTION AND NAPOLEONIC ERA FOR KIDS

THROUGH THE LIVES OF ROYALTY, REBELS, & THINKERS

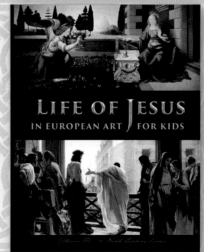

LIFE OF JESUS IN EUROPEAN ART FOR KIDS

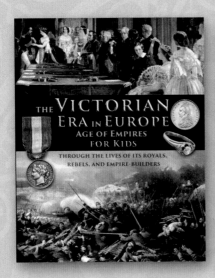

THE VICTORIAN ERA IN EUROPE
AGE OF EMPIRES FOR KIDS
THROUGH THE LIVES OF ITS ROYALS, REBELS, AND EMPIRE-BUILDERS

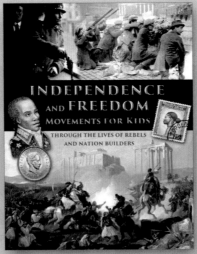

INDEPENDENCE AND FREEDOM MOVEMENTS FOR KIDS
THROUGH THE LIVES OF REBELS AND NATION BUILDERS

LATIN FOR KIDS

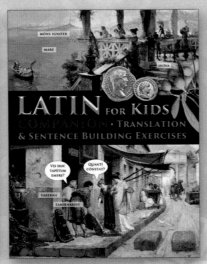

LATIN FOR KIDS
COMPANION · Translation & Sentence Building Exercises

LATIN TO THE RESCUE!
HOW TO MAKE SENSE OF ENGLISH SPELLING BY LEARNING A BIT OF LATIN

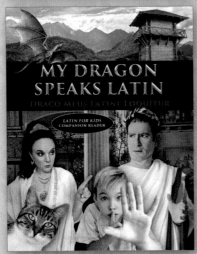

MY DRAGON SPEAKS LATIN
DRACO MEUS LATINE LOQUITUR
LATIN FOR KIDS COMPANION READER

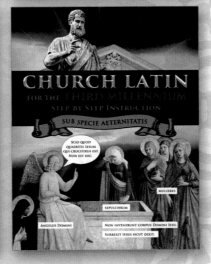

CHURCH LATIN FOR THE THIRD MILLENNIUM
STEP BY STEP INSTRUCTION
SUB SPECIE AETERNITATIS

Made in the USA
Middletown, DE
03 October 2024

61975900R00053